REFERENCES.
Market Days — *Mondays & Thursdays*
Fairs — *1st May, 2d November*

Post Miles from Poole.
To Wimborne 6
„ Christchurch 10
„ Ringwood 12
„ Wareham 9
„ Dorchester 25
„ Blandford 12
„ Swanage 20

Parish of St James, Coloured (also Ward) Yellow
  Do   Do   Do   Pink
  Do   Hamworthy   Do   White
  Do   Longfleet   Do   Green

Scale of Chains

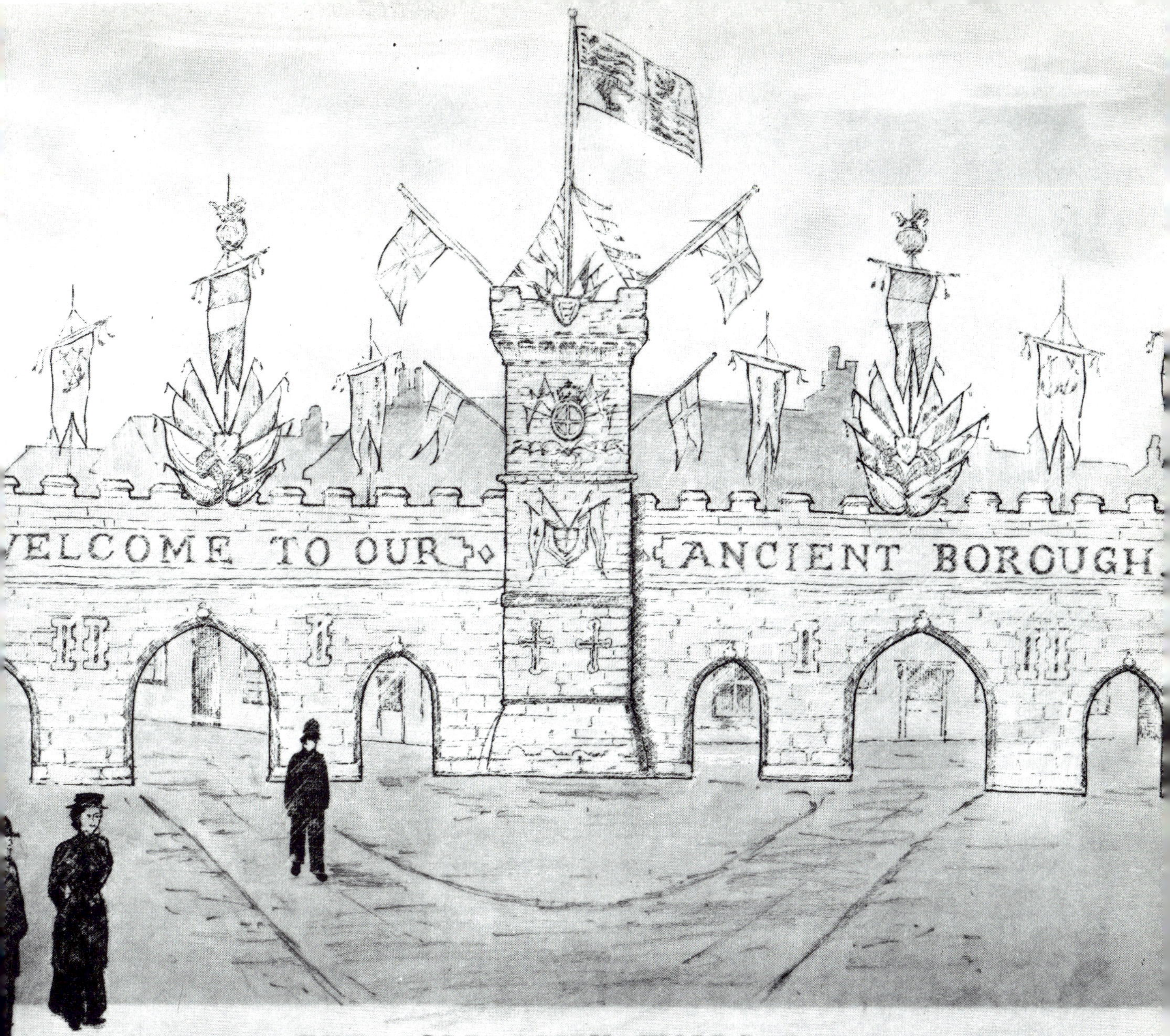

THE "OLD TOWN WALL," POOLE.

A Portfolio of Old Poole
by John Hillier

Poole Historical Trust—1983

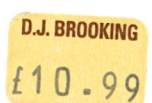

3rd August 2000

This volume is published by the Poole Historical Trust whose primary aims are the promotion of research into the publication of works on the history and life of Poole and the surrounding area.

Trustees

John Hillier, Chairman
Fred Rowe OBE, Vice Chairman
Ian Andrews MA (Oxon), Hon Secretary
Brian Elliott, Hon Treasurer
Martin Blyth
Brian Galpin
Andrew Hawkes
Graham Smith MA (RCA)

Previous Publications

Pride of Poole
An Album of Old Poole
Mansions and Merchants of Poole & Dorset
Brownsea Islander
Poole and World War II
Ebb-Tide at Poole
History of the Town and County of Poole 1839 (Reprint)
The Sydenhams of Poole (Pamphlet)
Art in Poole and Dorset
Poole After World War II
Victorian Poole
D-Day; Poole (Booklet)
Spirit of Poole
Lifeboatmen Never Turn Back
Schools of Old Poole
Poole's Pride Regained

© John Hillier, 1983

Reprinted July 1987
Reprinted March 1990
Reprinted June 1997

ISBN 0 9504914 2 X

All rights reserved. No part of this publication may be reproduced, stored in a retrieval system or transmitted in any form or by any means, electrical, mechanical, photocopying, recording or otherwise, without the permission of the copyright owner.

Photographic copying by Suzanne Sieger and Stanley Swain
Plans drawn by John Brixey
Index by Juliet Marlow ALA
Designed by Gordon Downland
Printed and bound in Great Britain by
Biddles Ltd, Guildford and King's Lynn

Contents

The Manor	Pages 6 – 15
The Precinct	16 – 37
High Street	38 – 49
Poole Park and its Royal Opening	50 – 59
The Quay	60 – 73
The Ham Ferry	
The Fishermen and their Fleet	
The Quay Railway	
The Quay in Wartime	
Quayside Types	
Poole Harbour	74 – 87
Old Harry Rocks	
South Haven Hotel	
Goathorn	
Some Famous Poole Ships	
Poole's Lifeboats	
Poole's Paddlesteamers	
Brownsea Island	
Communications	88 – 99
Poole's Royal Mail Coach	
The London & SW Railway	
Poole's old Railway Stations	
The Poole & District Electric Traction Company	
The Bournemouth Corporation Tramways	
Some other old Poole Streets	100 – 115
Parkstone	116 – 135
'The Village'	
Whitecliff	
Lilliput	
Canford Cliffs	
Sandbanks	
Longfleet	136 – 147
Branksome	148 – 155
Hamworthy	156 – 163
Broadstone	164 – 173
Index	174 – 176

Acknowledgments

I am very grateful to the many people who have helped in the compilation of this book either by the loan of photographs or plans, in furnishing information or in assistance in research, especially the following:

Bournemouth Corporation Transport; the Royal Commission on Historical Monuments (England); the Dorset County Reference Library; the Poole Reference Library; the Poole Corporation and Museums Service and the County Archivist of the West Sussex Record Office.

The Earl of Bessborough D. L.; Mrs R Allenby; Mr Roy Barter; Mrs R M Bird; Mr E H P Bristowe and his daughter Barbara; Mr John Fry; Mr Bill Harvey; Mr M Hayne; Mr H F V Johnstone; Mr Stanley Swain; Mr G V Van Schepdael and Mr Frank C Watkins.

I am also grateful to my colleague Derek Beamish, recently busy in obtaining a further degree in history, for reading through the MSS and for his help and suggestions.

Preface

John Sydenham wrote in the Preface to his *History of Poole*, published in 1838, 'Topography is, at best, an unpromising and unthankful branch of literature. Neither is the pecuniary return which is customarily its lot, nor in the reputation awarded to its student, does it offer any inducement to undertake that labour and expend that time which it rigidly requires.'

Despite the lack of such inducements, Poole has been fortunate in finding successors to John Sydenham, notably in H P Smith, in the research and writing of Poole's history. It has also been fortunate in having photographers, such as W J Day and E W Ralph before the First World War and, from 1932 onwards, Ernest Bristowe and his daughter Barbara, to take photographic records of older Poole.

Miss Barbara Bristowe and Mr Stanley Swain were commissioned by the Corporation to take photographs of Old Poole before the Slum Clearance and Redevelopment of Old Poole in the late 1950's and 1960's and some of their photographs are included in this collection as well as earlier photographs of W J Day, E W Ralph and many others.

Before the Bristowes emigrated some twenty years ago they made a collection of some 600 photographs, some of which were their own and some of which were copies of earlier ones. I have included many of these photographs in this volume and the Trust, with the help of the Poole Museums Service, has had copies of all the Bristowe collection made so that they might be put on inspection at the Poole Reference Library.

Also soon available will be a catalogue of all the 10,000 previously uncatalogued documents in the Corporation archives which the Trust has prepared under the direction of Derek Beamish and with the help of a Government Job Creation Scheme. This should add considerably to the information available to researchers.

Later in John Sydenham's Preface, he wrote that he had found the reward for his labours in his own interest and identification with the subject of his writings.

Happily, we find the same interest sufficient to motivate us today. We also find that a knowledge of what happened in the town in the past enhances the pleasure of living in or visiting it today. We hope our readers feel the same.

We are grateful for all the support we have received from those who have bought our books, for the help of our bankers and the booksellers of the region. It has allowed us to continue despite the recession and the enormous increase in the cost of producing our books.

2 Canford House from the river, 1890

The Manor

When Sir John Webb, the lord of the manor of Canford Magna and Poole, died in 1797 the old Burgesses of Poole could be forgiven for feeling considerable relief at the news. For decades they had been fighting Sir John in the courts over the ownership of reclaimed mudlands round the Quay and over rights of herbage and turbary over the vast 'wastes' of the manor.

Sir John was the last of a long line of Webbs who had ruled Canford since 1611. He had only one daughter, the Countess of Shaftesbury, and she herself had only one child, Lady Barbara Ashley. Thus Sir John, possibly feeling that neither of them would have need of his fortune, had left the manor to a sole trustee, Edward Arrowsmith, to accumulate its income until Lady Barbara's death. It was to be divided between his great grandchildren.

For a little while the 'Old Grey House', as the medieval manor house was known locally, remained empty, but soon Mr Arrowsmith had found a tenant in the Nuns of Hoogstraed, who came to England to 'avoid the excesses of the French Revolution'. Mr Arrowsmith had no wish to waste the manor's resources in litigation and a period of peace ensued between the Corporation and the manor. It was in this period that the Enclosure Acts were passed which allowed the Enclosure Commissioners to resolve all the outstanding quarrels. It allotted some 1,000 acres of the manor's land including the disputed mudlands to the Corporation in compensation for the extinguishment of all rights of common over the rest of the manor.

However, in 1824, Mr Arrowsmith died and a new trustee had to be appointed by the Court. Lady Barbara had married ten years earlier and, as it was her children who were the ultimate beneficiaries of Sir John's Will, the Court had no hesitation in appointing her husband, the Hon W F S Ponsonby, as the sole trustee.

It took the new lord very little time to decide that he and his family would live at Canford and that he would take an active part in the manor's affairs. It was, therefore, not long before the Nuns were taking ship at Poole Quay on their way back to the Continent and the old mansion house was being demolished to make room for a new 'Elizabethan-type' mansion more in keeping with the fortune now under the control of the acting lord of the manor.

Mr Ponsonby also had political ambitions and indicated to the Burgesses of Poole that he would be prepared to be one of the town's two Members of Parliament. The wily old merchants of Poole had always made a point of electing men who had influence at Westminster, especially if they were also wealthy enough to help the town substantially. Mr Ponsonby handsomely met both criteria. He promised to pay for the cost of erecting a library in High Street on land to be given by Poole's other MP, – and there could be no doubt as to his influence in Parliament for his father was the Earl of Bessborough and his aunt was none other than the Duchess of Devonshire, the *grande dame* of the Whig aristocracy. He even had access to the Whig cabinet in that his brother was a member of it and his sister Caroline had married William Lamb, another Whig Minister, who was shortly afterwards to become Viscount Melbourne and later Prime Minister. Mr Ponsonby was duly elected as Poole's junior MP in 1826.

But, in electing Mr Ponsonby the Burgesses of Poole had made one desperately wrong assumption. They had assumed that as their MP he would use his influence at Westminster on their behalf. It was not long afterwards that he made his position quite clear to them when, in total opposition to the Tory majority of the Corporation, he strongly supported the Reform Bill. The Poole Corporation strenuously opposed the passing of the Bill but to no avail.

After that Mr Ponsonby probably felt that his chances of re-election as Poole's MP were not good. Whatever the reason, he suddenly resigned his seat to stand for election against Lord Ashley, then entrenched in his Dorset constituency. He would score a notable victory for the Whigs if he was able to unseat Lord Ashley, and Mr Ponsonby bent every effort to this end. However, as the leisurely assessment of the validity of votes proceeded at Dorchester, it became evident that Mr Ponsonby was going to be thwarted by an odd vote or two. Immediately, before the result was declared, a sudden tirade of accusations and threats was issued by Mr Ponsonby and his supporters against everyone who had been involved in the election. The Dorset Under-Sheriff had disqualified himself from acting by declaring his support for Lord Ashley; the Clerk of the Council was 'nothing but the paid agent of Lord Ashley'; the Assessors had acted wrongly in allowing votes which had been cast 'by mere squatters on common land'. They had even allowed votes to count which had been cast by mere inmates of Almshouses at Wimborne and Weymouth! There would, thundered the lord of the manor, be a House of Commons investigation.

The Burgesses of Poole would have done well to have heeded the events in Dorchester but, at the time, the country was in the ferment of the contraversies over the Reform Bills and they had other things to worry about, not least their waning Newfoundland trade. It was, too, around this time that the Boundary Commissioners arrived in Poole to consider whether any boundary changes should be made prior to any future elections under the Reform Bills. The Poole Corporation suggested that it might be well to extend the borough boundaries to include that part of Hamworthy near the Quays and to incorporate a part of Longfleet which contained the town's small overspill population. It was a proposal which the Commissioners accepted and they incorporated it into their recommendations to the Government. But when the provisions of the Boundary Act became known in Poole it was found that, not only had the whole of Hamworthy and Longfleet been added to Poole, but also the whole of the large tithing of Parkstone.

The horrified Burgesses had little doubt as to who had engineered this absurdly large extension of the boundaries of the little borough. Everyone living in these added areas was a tenant of the manor and, with no secret ballot in the proposed voting system, it meant that few of those qualified to vote in the additional areas would be brave or foolish enough to vote contrary to the lord's wishes. The lord of the manor had stolen an advantage which could well prove crucial in any future election.

In fact it was eventually found that under the new franchise out of a total population of some 8,000 people in the newly extended borough only 412 men were entitled to vote and they were almost equally divided in their support of the Tories and the Reform candidates. The very first municipal elections in Poole in 1835, therefore, ended with a result very similar to the one in Dorchester – the Tories were declared to have won a very narrow majority. As soon as the results were declared in Poole there followed an almost repeat performance of the events and accusations which had followed the Dorset election.

'Capt' George Parrott, an eager henchman of the lord of the manor and the newly-elected leader of the Reformers, had always warned his supporters that the Tory merchants would somehow cheat them of their deserts. They immediately alleged that the elections had been rigged by Robert Parr, the old Burgesses's town clerk. Then they complained that Thomas Arnold, the new town clerk, had allowed them insufficient time to examine the ballot papers. They issued a Writ designed to get the High Court to order that they should be allowed sufficient time with the ballot papers to check and recount them. They served a Writ on two of the newly elected Councillors summoning them to attend the Dorset Assizes to show on what authority they were acting as Councillors and waggon-loads of voters, who together formed a majority in that Ward, were carted off to Dorchester so that all eighty-eight of them could swear that they had voted for the two losing candidates! Meanwhile, the Member of Parliament for Shaftesbury had persuaded the House of Commons to set up a Select

Committee to inquire into and report on the election in Poole. Then, to round off the first fusilage of shots, Mr Ponsonby himself served a High Court writ on the new Council alleging that its agreement to pay compensation to Mr Parr, the previous town clerk, for loss of office under the Municipal Corporations Act, was illegal.

As if this early reaction of the Reformers and their 'Paymaster at Canford' was not enough, Lord John Russell, the Home Secretary, then made sure that the municipal affairs of Poole were reduced to complete farce. He reconstituted the Bench of Magistrates by accepting the six nominees of the Poole Reformers, rejecting all the nominees of the ruling Tory party on the Council. The effect of this was that the Council was effectively stopped from collecting any rates for the new Bench of Magistrates promptly dismissed all summonses brought before them to enforce payment!

The proceedings of the Council were soon reduced to tragicomedy. Only by mortgaging its properties could it meet even its most pressing day-to-day expenses. Its new town clerk was using his own money to pay the immense costs of the litigation. Mr Parr, the earlier town clerk, meanwhile obtained judgment for the payment of the first instalment of his compensation and, at his behest, the court issued distraint on all the 'personal' effects of the Corporation. The Bailiffs seized all the old seals and the maces, even its newly-acquired Guildhall furniture, and sold them at auction. Not long afterwards the High Court transferred all the Corporation's property to Mr Parr so that he could receive the rents towards the payment of his judgment debts. The Corporation was then unable even to raise money by the mortgage of its property.

By this time the Corporation had not enough money even to maintain and feed its prisoners in the Town Gaol who then were left to rely on the benevolence of the Sheriff. The poor, too, were left dependent on the personal charity of the Overseers, for the Poor Rate had been amalgamated with the General Rate, payment of which had been effectively stopped by the Magistrates. Then, to make the Council's disarray complete, the health of Mr Arnold, their town clerk, began to fail under the stress of those ten years of constant crisis. He still had not been repaid any of the court costs which he had incurred on behalf of the Council so, as he resigned, he took all the Corporation's deeds, documents and papers by way of lien for the costs which the Corporation owed him. He then brought an action against the Corporation for the recovery of these costs. The court inquired into these costs and assessed that the Corporation owed Mr Arnold £11,124. 4s. 0d – an amount some fourteen times greater than the total of the General Rate which the Corporation was then vainly trying to collect and a sum equal to about £275,000 at today's values.

If the Corporation had had the ability to go bankrupt it would long before have been declared insolvent. As it was the outrageous use of the lord of the manor's wealth through the courts to intimidate the opposition on the one hand was evenly matched by the dogged hatred of the old Tory merchants and the remorseless Mr Parr on the other. After ten years of conflict there were no signs that either side was relenting.

At last, however, fate intervened. Lady de Mauley (Mr Ponsonby had been created Lord de Mauley in 1838) died and, with her death, the Canford wealth was suddenly snatched from Lord de Mauley. His trusteeship came to an end as the estate went into the Court of Exchequer for the trust to be wound up and the property divided between Lady de Mauley's children.

While the Court came to its leisurely decisions as to the winding-up of the trust and putting the manor of Canford up for sale a wonderful transformation came over the relationships in the Borough in the absence of the lord of the manor. The implacable Mr Parr finally won his case against Lord de Mauley in the House of Lords. The Reformers, then in power in the Council, won their case against his successor, Mr Arnold, on the slender ground that he had failed to get the Corporation's seal put on his instructions to bring or defend the court proceedings. The Corporation was eventually able to complete its sale of the advowson of the Church of St James and to raise a loan from the Economic Assurance Co to meet its judgment debts, albeit at the price of having to repay it by half-yearly instalments until 1865. Then, as they awaited their new lord of the manor, they had time to put their affairs into some sort of order.

About this time the Whigs had adopted the Reformers into their reconstituted Party and the combined Party had become known as the Liberal Party. It must therefore have been with some apprehension that the old Tory merchants heard that their new lord of the manor was already a Liberal member of Parliament. He was Sir J J Guest, 'the great ironmaster of Dowlais' who had been persuaded by his wife, Lady Charlotte, to buy the property. He paid £335,000 for it but, even so, they felt that they could not occupy it before it had been 'adapted' for their use, an 'adaption' which entailed the building of the Great Hall, a library and the tower. They commissioned Sir Charles Barry to carry out the additions and adaptions. A leading architect of the time, he some years earlier, had won the competition for the rebuilding of the Houses of Parliament.

However, the delay in the Guests' occupation of Canford House was well worth waiting for because as soon as they had come to Canford it was clear that relationships between the new lord of the manor and his workmen, tenants and the Poole Corporation was going to be very different from what they had been. Canford Park was opened up for cricket matches, the Manor held Agricultural Shows and Richard Ledgard, the Conservative Mayor of Poole, was a frequent guest at Canford House.

Sir John at this time even contemplated changing his allegiance from his Merthyr constituency to Poole and discussed the possibility with Mr Kemp Welch, the Liberal Agent, and with George Parrott, its leader. Sir John was probably glad that he had made no precipitous decision to stand for Poole when, a little later, he watched a Poole hustings from Mr Mooring Aldridge's office at the side of the Guildhall. It was soon evident that the old Poole emnities had not been all assuaged for Mr Parrott was pasted with eggs and exploding bags of flour as he started to expound the virtues of his candidate and the two factions fell on each other in strenuous combat.

However, these remnants of the violent political passions of Poole were never allowed to mar the unique relationship which sprang up between the town and their new lord but, unfortunately, they never had time to flourish. After only two years at Canford Sir John Guest died. His heir, Sir Ivor Bertie Guest, was then only 17 years old and Lady Charlotte was left with the great responsibilities of the ironworks at Dowlais (which she took so seriously that it was said that she learnt to speak nine languages to help forward the sales) as well as of bringing up her ten children. She was, therefore, often away from Canford, and had little time for the affairs of the manor which were left to Mr Luff, her steward. Then, three years after the death of Sir John, Lady Charlotte married her son's tutor, Charles Schreiber, while Sir Ivor was still at Cambridge.

It was not, therefore, until August, 1856, when Sir Ivor came of age, that Canford once again had its lord of the manor. Canford went *en fete* for the occasion. In the morning the tenants made their new lord a presentation of plate and then over a thousand guests sat down to lunch in a large marquee erected in the grounds. In the afternoon children from all parts of the lord's great estate were entertained with games and races among the fountains as the bands in the park vied with the pealing of the church bells, and acrobat and Punch-and-Judy shows were followed by tea. Then, in the evening it was their elders' turn as a Ball was held in Canford House for over 800 guests. It was a glittering occasion with Mrs Schreiber coming out of mourning for the first time since the death of Sir John in a white silk dress relieved with red roses, and once again wearing her diamonds and rubies. Outside on the lawns, the fountains were illuminated and during the interval in the dancing, there was a grand display of fireworks. It was 6 a.m. next morning before the bands finally played 'God Save the Queen'.

It was an altogether new way for the tenants and workmen to welcome a new lord to the manor. Everyone left Canford that night feeling that a new and brighter era had begun. But they were premature. Sir Ivor, the new lord, was still a young man who was far from ready to settle down at Canford as the lord of the manor. His interests were elsewhere, in Wales, in Scotland and in travelling on the Continent. In 1862, for instance, he was made a Justice of the Peace of Glamorgan and, shortly afterwards, was appointed High Sheriff of Ross-shire.

For all that, though, he did keep a regular connection with Canford. He returned each summer for the Horticultural Show in Canford Park, for the tennis tournaments and shooting parties which he organised for his friends. At these times, too, his mother and step-father were regular visitors to Canford. The family, too, enjoyed amateur theatricals for which they had been given a taste on their visits to the exuberant Col. and Mrs Waugh at Brownsea Island. Indeed Sir Ivor later had bought the lavish stage, scenery and props at the sale at Brownsea after the Colonel had absconded to Spain and his creditors had sold off what assets he had left on the island. Sir Ivor and his mother had, too, set up a private printing press at Canford on which they produced original editions of books which included the first edition of poems by Lady Charlotte's friend, Sir Alfred Tennyson.

But it was not until after Sir Ivor's marriage in 1868 to Lady Cornelia Churchill, the eldest daughter of the Duke of Marlborough, that he took over his responsibilities as lord of the manor and made Canford House his home.

The vivacious and extrovert Lady Cornelia who then came to Canford was generally given the credit for the fruitful period of help and co-operation between the lord of the manor and the Corporation. Sir Ivor himself (made Baron Wimborne of Canford Magna in 1880 by his friend Lord Beaconsfield at the end of his last term of office as Prime Minister) was himself a generous man as well as a kind landlord.

He and Lady Cornelia were greatly involved in the provision of many of the churches erected at this time at Broadstone and in Upper and Lower Parkstone. It was he, too, who made possible the schools at Broadstone and Longfleet. It was also Lord Wimborne who was responsible for the golf courses at Broadstone and Parkstone. He first had the course at Broadstone constructed for the use of himself and his friends, but soon residents of Broadstone were being invited to use the course and Lady Cornelia did much to encourage women to take part in the sport. Later, it was Lord Wimborne again who developed the course at Parkstone. He exchanged part of the land previously used by the Longfleet Rope Works, known locally as The 'Ladies' Walking Field (now forming part of the Arndale Centre, bus station and car park), for the disused reservoirs and pumping house of the Poole Waterworks Company which the Corporation had taken over and abandoned. He added this land of the old waterworks to his adjoining land to form the course. He was its first President and his younger brother Freddie Guest, Winston Churchill's cousin and friend, was the first captain of the Club. Lord Wimborne also took an active part in local politics, first of all in Broadstone and later in Poole where, in 1896, he became the first person to be made Mayor of Poole who had not first served his apprenticeship as a Councillor.

But it was his wife, Lady Cornelia, who was the driving force. Mr P E L Budge, the solicitor agent of the Conservatives in Poole and its Mayor on two occassions, once said of her that 'she had an irresistable means of getting her own way which should cause any man who did not agree with her to fly to the uttermost ends of the earth'!

Certainly it was she who has generally been given the credit of the ready exchange of lands with the manor which allowed the formation of what became to be known as Parkstone Park as well as the gift of land for the formation of Poole Park for which Lord & Lady Wimborne are best remembered. It was, too, typical of her that when Lord Wimborne attended the Sheriff's meeting to consider what memorial Poole should provide to mark the Jubilee of Queen Victoria's reign, he attended to propose that it should be in the form of a cottage hospital. He promised the gift of an appropriate house and, he said, Lady Cornelia had promised to give £1,000 of the £5,000 that he estimated it would require to alter and equip it. The meeting did not consider that Poole could raise such a large sum as £4,000 and the vote of the meeting went to Mr J J Norton's proposition that the memorial should take the form of a free library.

From the lack of financial support for the Library Fund it is clear that the doubts then expressed at the meeting were well founded. However, undeterred, Lady Cornelia proceeded herself to establish the 'Cornelia Hospital', a name which was retained long after it was moved to Longfleet and which it lost only when the National Health Service provided the present building of the Poole General Hospital.

Those halcyon days of the generous involvement of the lord of the manor in Poole's affairs did not survive the death of Lord Wimborne in 1914. His son, Ivor Churchill Guest, already a peer in his own right as Baron Ashby St Leger and, at the time of his father's death, Lord in Waiting to George V, succeeded his father. The following year he was appointed Lord Lieutenant of Ireland, a post he retained until the end of the war in 1918, when he was created Viscount Wimborne.

By the time of his father's death, however, the new lord of the manor had lost any interest he might ever have had in Canford or in being its lord, but he did nothing to disturb his family at Canford until after Lady Cornelia's death in 1927. After his mother's death, however, he wanted no part in the manor's previous involvement in the affairs of the district. Those parts of the estate which were financially unproductive were put up for sale. The golf courses were examples of this. In 1928 it was proposed to abandon the Parkstone course and sell off the land for housing development. It was only saved as a golf course by Mr W T Simpson, the developer of Compton Acres Gardens, who just managed with the help of friends to beat the deadline for its purchase so that it could be retained as a golf course. Then, a few years later, a purchaser was found for Canford House itself which, with its park, was sold for the establishment of Canford School.

The rest of the still extensive estate of the old manor was left in the capable hands of agents to administer as best they could in the financial interests of the absentee landlord. The new lord of the manor had inherited none of the concerns of his parents for the people whose industry made his land more and more valuable. Soon all local feelings of almost reverence which had grown between the people of Poole and their lord and lady at Canford turned to suspicion and distrust. It was, it seemed, not an unusual feeling in regard to the Viscount Wimborne, for H P Belloc had uncharacteristically written a bitter little poem about him which ran

> Grant, O Lord, eternal rest
> To thy servant, Ivor Guest,
> Never mind the where or how,
> Only grant it to him now.

The Golden Age of the generous help by the manor to those living within its boundaries had passed into history. It was therefore a curious turn of fate when a few years later the Poole Corporation, the successors of the old Burgesses who had fought for centuries to extract from the lord of the manor enough powers to administer their little town, took over the administration of Canford as Broadstone and Canford joined the Borough in 1935.

Meanwhile few mementos remain in Poole of Lady Cornelia and her indulgent husband who had done so much for the town. The Cornelia Working Men's Club, the Cornelia Hospital and the rest have gone or been forgotten. Only Cornelia Cresent near Guest Avenue and Winston Avenue remain as small reminders of the unique lord and lady of the Manor of Canford Magna and Poole.

3 Sir J J Guest, 1785 – 1852. Sir John's grandfather had established the iron works at Dowlais in 1758. Sir John was MP for Honiton, 1825-31 and for Merthyr Tydfyl from 1832-52. He was made a baronet in 1838, five years after he had married Lady Charlotte Bertie, daughter of the Earl of Lindsay. He bought the manor in September, 1845.

4 Lady Charlotte Guest, 1812 – 1895. An ardent Liberal but her second husband, Charles Shreiber, was an active Conservative. In the 1880 General Election her husband and two of her sons stood as Conservative candidates and two other sons put up as Liberal candidates. Her husband was elected at Poole with a majority of 6. Her son Montague was elected for the adjoining constituency of Wareham. Her collection of porcelain, 'the Shreiber Collection', forms the basis of the Victoria and Albert Museum's collection. She presented the Lectern to St James Church, Poole, in memory of Charles Shreiber. In 1888 she contracted glaucoma and went blind.

5   Cricket match at Canford House in the 1850's

6 Block plan of Canford House, 1850. Sir Charles Barry's plan of Canford House after his additions and alterations. There was a serious fire at Canford House in 1884 when the main staircase was destroyed and many fine tapestries, paintings and china were ruined. This was just before Charles Shreiber's death and subsequent burial at Canford Church. In 1887 Lord Wimborne added a new wing.

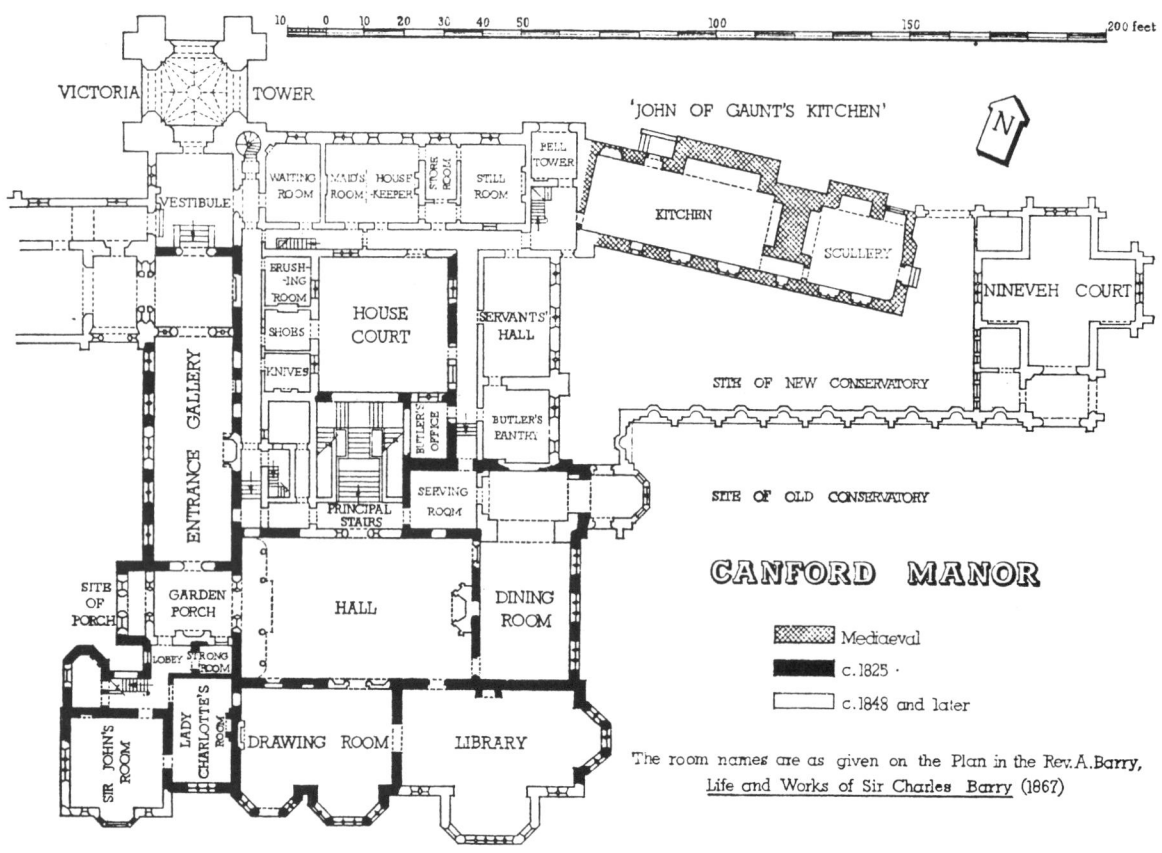

7 Canford House from the south-west, 1890. The manor's lands comprised over 16,000 acres and included Little Canford, Ensbury, Kinson, Knighton, Longfleet, Merley, Parkstone and Upton as well as Canford Magna and Poole.

8 Baron Wimborne of Canford Magna, 1835 – 1914. Married Lady Cornelia Churchill in 1868. Lord of the manor for 58 years. For many years the Chairman of the Broadstone Parish Council. Mayor of Poole in 1896.

9 Lady Cornelia Wimborne, 1890. Lady Cornelia was the eldest daughter of John Winston, 7th Duke of Marlborough, Lord President in Disraeli's cabinet. She was an eloquent speaker, reputed never to speak at less than 150 words a minute. During her tenure at Canford there was a constant procession of royal guests and ruling statesmen as well as frequent Conservative fetes, Horticultural Shows, Tennis tournaments, cricket matches and shooting parties. At one Primrose League gathering in 1885 it was said that over 30,000 people attended – among 'torrents of rain'. The Press at her death in January, 1927, described her as 'popular', 'the beloved lady' and commended her 'cheery disposition'. Her son 'Freddy' Guest, Winston Churchill's friend, was MP for East Dorset (then including Poole) at the time of her death

10 The Library at Canford House

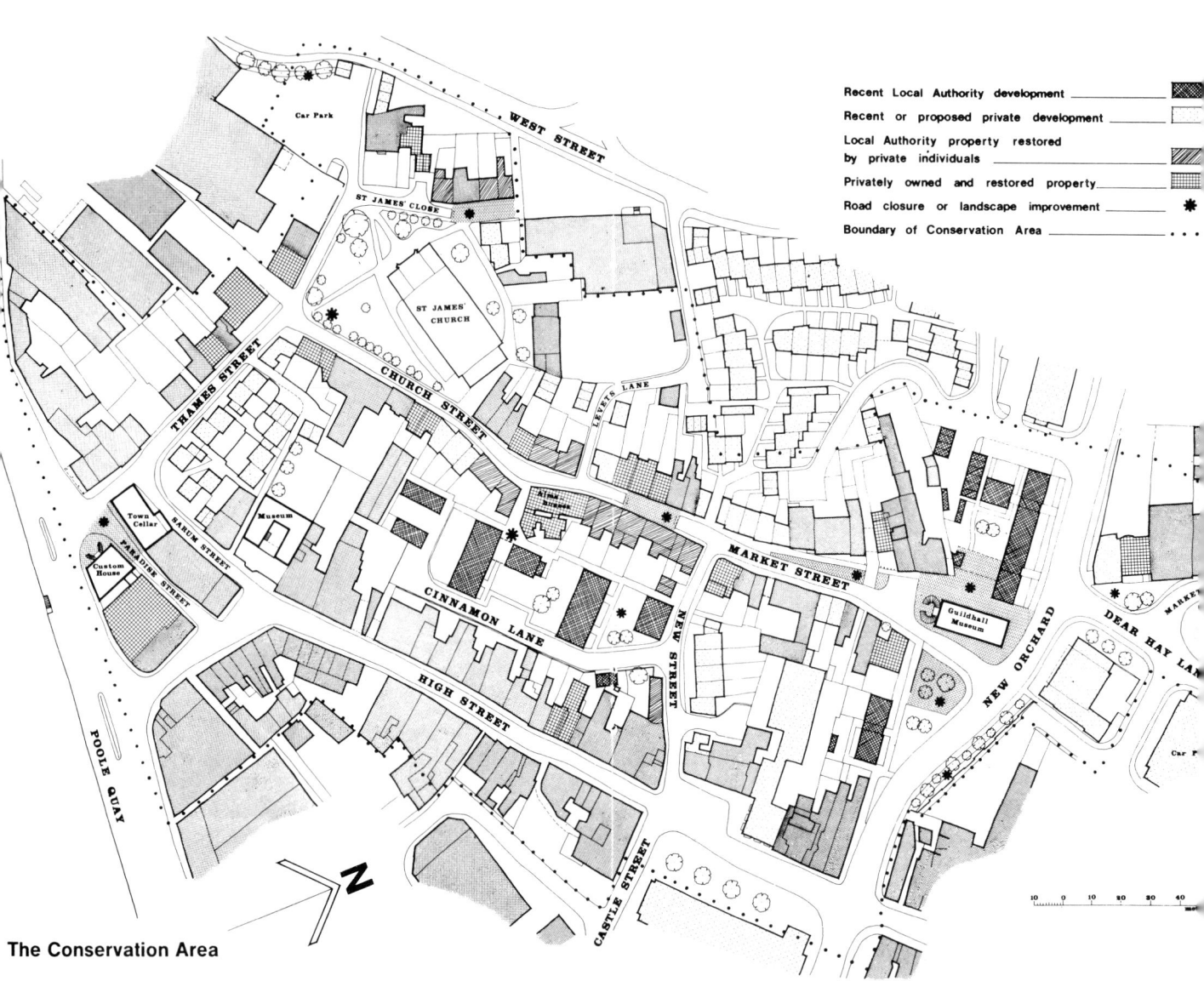

The Conservation Area

11 The Precinct

The Precinct

One of the more difficult problems of the Slum Clearance and Redevelopment of Old Poole was how to deal with the many buildings which had been listed as having some feature of historical or architectural merit. Most of them were in a ruinous condition, and all of them were set tight upon the little horse-and-cart streets or lanes of Old Poole. Owners could be given no incentive to rehabilitate such houses which would inevitably become isolated and incongruously situate among any possible redevelopment.

The only hope of preserving part of Poole's heritage of old buildings, it was decided, was to take an area in which all houses capable of restoration could be rehabilitated, where the old road pattern could be retained, where non-conforming uses could be removed and a whole area restored in such a way that people would again wish to live in it.

The obvious location for such a zone was the area lying west of the bottom of High Street and between the Quay and the Guildhall. There were many substantial old buildings in this area including six of the twelve old mansion houses of Old Poole (13 Thames Street, 11 & 32 West Street, West End House and 6 & 8 New Street) and the area also included such important public buildings as St James Church, the Custom House, Scaplen's Court and the Guildhall.

Following this decision, the Corporation made the 'Poole Town Comprehensive Development Order' in 1960 and, in the written statement accompanying the order, the Corporation set out its aims. "The primary object of this zone", it wrote, "is to preserve the heritage of old buildings of special architectural or historical interest in the Old Town, not as individual buildings in isolation but in groups, sufficient in number effectively to preserve the street scene as their rightful setting."

The clearance of the slums and the rehousing of the displaced familes was the first priority of the Corporation. It was therefore not until 1964 that the work of establishing the Precinct could proceed. It started with a detailed survey of all the properties comprised in the Redevelopment Area. The results of this survey were most disappointing. The condition of most of the properties was even worse than had been thought. A Sub-Committee of the Corporation, after inspecting the area, felt that there was no alternative but to abandon the project.

However, the Council had made its comprehensive development order on the basis of its total scheme for the Old Town and decided that every effort should be made to bring it into effect. The houses shown in the survey to be beyond all hope of possible restoration were condemned, compulsorily purchased and demolished. The owners of commercial and industrial premises in the area were offered alternative sites on the Corporation's industrial estate. Most of the remaining houses of the area were declared unfit for human occupation and were made the subject of Closing Orders. On the confirmation of these Orders the Corporation offered to purchase the properties as an alternative to the owners carrying out the necessary work of rehabilitating them. It was an offer which most owners were only too happy to accept.

The properties which the Corporation bought in this way were offered on long lease to any applicant willing to undertake the extensive work required to bring them up to modern living standards. The Corporation offered to make Improvement Grants to applicants and, as Building Societies were reluctant to lend money on the security of such old and run down property, the Corporation offered to advance the necessary money in phased instalments as the work proceeded to its satisfaction. At first only one or two of the Corporation's own architects had sufficient faith in the scheme to take on the challenge but soon, as soon as it was seen what could be done, others came forward with schemes to restore the houses of the Precinct.

About a dozen owners opted to restore their own property and, in some of these cases the Corporation was able to help in making extra land available to improve the curtelages and air space around the houses or to provide space for garages. The two criteria of all plans was that the outside appearance of the houses should be preserved and that their interiors should be brought up to modern standards.

After the demolition of the properties incapable of being restored there was a considerable area of vacant land and private enterprise did a great deal to bring about the success of the venture. The odd infilling of houses in conformity with the Precinct at the corner of Church Street and Thames Street, in the Church Street frontage of the old scrap yard and at the corner of Church Street and Levet's Lane were all accomplished by private enterprise. It was private builders, too, who built the town houses on the area formerly occupied by the old warehouses and public lavatory in Thames Street as well as the houses fronting on to Market Street from the Wessex Industries' site.

The Corporation itself, having cleared the small cottages and industrial users from Cinnamon Lane, was able to afford extra land for the back of houses in Church Street as well as to provide rear access for the properties in High Street. It then used the remaining land to build a block of 34 flats, most of which were specially designed for elderly people.

Then, later, in 1969, the Corporation built the Guildhall Court Flats on the site of the entrance to the closed King Street and the Old Greyhound Inn and Wellington House (see photos 54 & 55). At the same time Market Street was closed to vehicular traffic at this point, enclosing the Precinct from the new New Orchard Road (it took its name from the previous New Orchard which had led from High Street to Market Street below the Guildhall and which had been closed (photo 69).

While the work of restoration was going on the Corporation relaid the water, electricity and gas services in the streets of the area prior to reconstructing the roadways. The gas lamps of the old Corporation were converted to electric operation and reintroduced into the Precinct. The pavements were relaid with riven slate tiles to encourage a 'Georgian' look to the area. Then, to complete the transformation, the old Guildhall, itself then in almost as sorry a state as its surrounding property, was given a complete overhaul and converted into a Museum.

By this time the area had achieved a character of its own and had come alive again as many people now wished to live in it. The Corporation was awarded the Gold Medal for Good Design by the Minister of Housing and Local Government in 1970. It also obtained a Civic Trust Award. Then, Poole because of its success with its Precinct was chosen, with Chester, as the two representatives of England at the European Architectural Heritage Year in 1975.

11b The Ministry of Housing's Gold Medal for design, 1970

Paradise Street–The Town Cellars

12 The Town Cellars, 1870. Listed under the Ancient Monuments Act as a building the preservation of which is of national importance. It seems likely that this building was erected in the first half of the 15th century after Poole had been made a Port of the Staple by Henry VI in 1433 and first used as a store for wool brought into the town from the extensive sheep-rearing areas of Dorset. It is styled 'The Woolhouse' in Poole's earliest records and later became known as 'The King's Hall'. The building to the right of the Town Cellars was the Ship Inn, demolished by Messrs Oakley, corn merchants in 1871. In 1692 it was called 'The Paradice Cellars' and later converted into the White Hart Inn. In 1820 it was known as the Coal Exchange public house before it was finally named the Ship Inn.

13 The Town Cellars and Warehouse, 1950. Messrs Oakley built the warehouse on the site of the Ship Inn. It was acquired by the Corporation during the redevelopment period by way of exchange for land on which Roger's House is built in New Orchard. The warehouse was acquired for the eventual extension of the Maritime Museum which was established in the Town Cellars.

Paradise Street – The Quay

14 The Old Town Water Pump, 1958. Inscribed 'John Strong, 1809'. The protective covering was presented by the Society of Poole Men in 1929. Paradise Street was formerly known as 'Paradice Row' a name which is thought to have been a corruption of the original 'route par Adieux' (Farewell Street) The photograph shows clearly how the Town Cellars was originally much longer before Thames Street was cut through it.

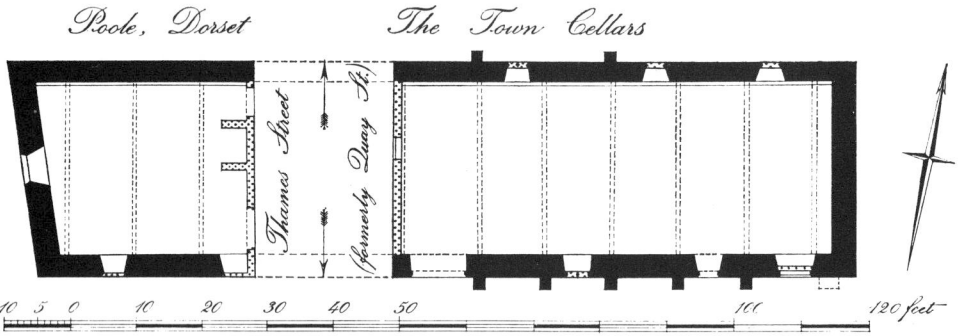

15 Ground plan of the original Town Cellars. The cut off portion is now owned by the brewers as part of the King Charles public house which adjoins the cut-off portion. The Town Cellars are shown still entire in a plan of 1768.

16 The Colonnade, Harbour Office, 1949. The Harbour Office was built in 1727 in front of what was to become the cut-off portion of the Town Cellars. It was built by the merchants of the town as a place of resort and provided with newspapers, maps and charts. In 1822 the merchants obtained the permission of the Corporation to extend the first floor of the building six feet out on to the Quay supported by columns.

The Quay

17 THE HARBOUR OFFICE, 1949. Over the side entrance is a bass relief of Benjamin Scutt in whose mayoralty the clubhouse was founded. He presented to it what was said to be a very fine portrait of Charles II which he had inherited from his grandfather who had attended Charles II on his formal visit to Poole. It hung over the fireplace of the Harbour Office for many years and later in the Guildhall. The building has recently been taken over by H M Coastguards.

18 The Sundial, Harbour Office. A memorial to Samuel Weston. He was the seventh member of the Weston family to be Mayor of Poole between 1710 and 1814. The family had always owned one-fourteenth share in the premises. The original ornamental balustrade can be seen in this older photograph.

19 THE CUSTOM HOUSE. The Custom House was originally built in the late 1700's facing along the Great Quay. It took the place of the Red Lion Coffee House. After the realignment of the quays in 1788 it overlooked the triangular area of open space which was then formed. In April 1813 it was destroyed by fire and the present building was erected soon afterwards to the plans of the original building.

Cinnamon Lane

20 Nos. 4, 5 and 6 Cinnamon Lane. Cinnamon Lane ran round the back of houses in Market Street to lead into New Street. No. 6, the house with the mansard roof, was built in the early 1600's; the other houses later that century.

21 Cinnamon Lane led into New Street opposite No. 8 New Street.

22 The Old Ostler's Stables and Yard, 1959. The cobbled stones of the original stables remained intact but the building had suffered greatly from neglect and the ravages of time. The New Antelope Inn lay to its right.

Sarum Street – Scaplen's Court

23 H P Smith MBE JP BA FCP, 1892 – 1953. Mr. Smith published two volumes of his proposed three-volume history of Poole. He died before he could complete the work. He had come to Poole from Leicester in 1913 as a teacher at South Road School and had become its Headmaster in 1926. He later moved to Henry Harben School when that school was built.

24 Scaplen's Court from Salisbury Street, 1923. A group of tenement building were wrecked in a gale in 1923. The walls and roof of an earlier building round which the tenements had been built were exposed. After an inspection Mr. Smith was convinced he had found the 'fair town house of stone by the kay' which Leland had described on his visit to Poole between 1536 and 1542.

25 Scaplen's Court from the courtyard, 1923. Mr. Smith persuaded the Society of Poole Men to buy the wrecked building. The Corporation bought the building in 1931 but, in 1950, it was found to be unsafe and it remained closed until 1959 while extensive works of restoration were completed.

26 Scaplen's Court from the courtyard, 1959. The building after its restoration. In the 17th century it was the George Inn. Later it had been the home of John Scaplen, Sheriff of Poole in 1773 and from whom it took its name. It was opened as one of the Corporation's museums in May, 1959.

Thames Street – South West side

| The Quay | The old Harbour Office | Town Cellars (divided part) | King's Head | St Clement's Lane | Nos 5 & 7 |

27 Thames Street in 1885. Previously known as Quay Street, Thames Street leads between the two parts of the Town Cellars from the Quay to what was the junction of Barber's Piles and West Street. West Street used to run northwards at right angles from this junction. The New Inn (now the King Charles) was built as a house in the late 1500's and was used as such until its conversion into an inn in 1770. At the shop to its immediate right Sally Betts used to sell Sunday dinners to families leaving matins at St James on Sundays for one penny.

28 The Water Gate. Approached now through the coach entrance of No. 5 Thames Street, the old St. Clement's Inn. The water gate was long thought to have been part of the original seaward fortifications of the town. St. Clements Lane, seen through the doorway, leads to the Quay.

29 The Water Gate. Dr. W Turner argued cogently in a lecture in 1887 that the wall, less thick than ordinary house walls of the period, and with steps to the battlement too narrow to allow a man-at-arms to mount were, in fact, the outer walls of a Nunnery established around 1250 by Abbess Ela, the widow of the lord of the manor, and which was decimated by the Black Death in 1348. Dr. Turner produced many arguments towards showing that the Nunnery covered a considerable area of ground including the Town Cellars which, he suggested, was the original chapel of the Convent of St. Clements. Nothing definite has ever been found to support his theories.

Thames Street – South West side

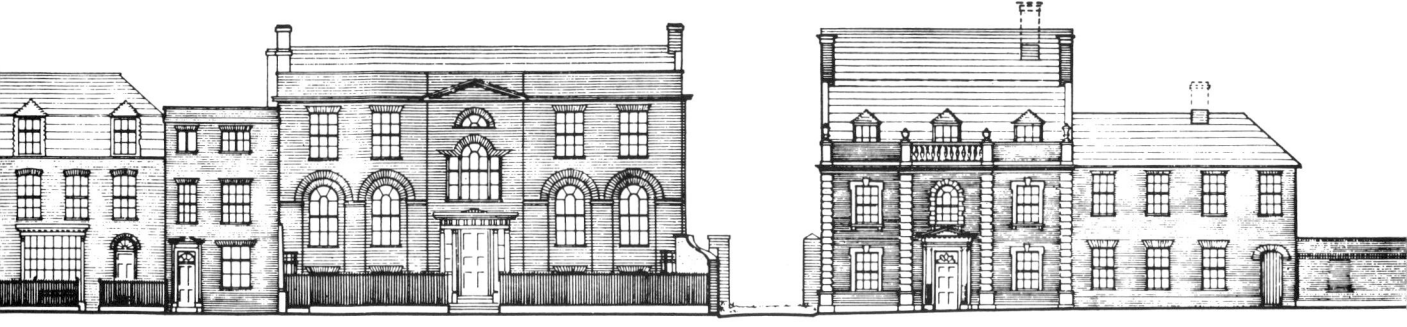

No 9   No 10   The Mansion House   No 13

Two of Poole's Mansion Houses

30 The Mansion House. Built by John Swetland, a Poole Builder, for Isaac Lester, a notable Newfoundland merchant. Isaac Lester died in 1778 before the building was completed. It was taken over by his brother Benjamin Lester, an MP for Poole and a friend of the Prime Minister, Lord North. Benjamin Lester was a leading advocate of the punitive measures being taken against the American colonists which precipitated their revolution. Benjamin Lester left his property to his grandson Lester Garland, subject to this adopting the surname of Lester.

After the war the property was used as a lodging house until it was taken over by Mr. Arthur Coates who, with his nephew Jurgens, refurbished the building and converted it into a members' dining club and hotel. It is now the Mansion House Club.

31 Poole House. Built about 1750 by the Weston family, it was later bought by Robert Slade, another Newfoundland merchant. From about 1952 it was owned by John Harper & Co Ltd and was saved from demolition by the Corporation agreeing that its interior could be convered for use by the workmen of the adjoining iron foundry subject to the appearance of the building not being altered.

Thames Street – Church Street

32 The corner of Thames Street and Church Street, 1958. Thames Alley ran from Thames Street into Hancock's Alley which led into Sarum Street at the side of Scaplen's Court. These properties were included in one of the later Clearance Areas of the Corporation.

33 1, 3 & 5 Church Street, 1958. No. 1 Church Street was demolished and replaced by a cottage type residence set back from the corner. Nos. 3 & 5 Church Street were able to be rehabilitated and together formed the Poole residence of the then MP for Poole, Mr. Oscar Murton, now Lord Murton. The photograph was taken through the Mansion House railings.

34 1, 3 & 5 Church Street after the rebuilding of No. 1 and the restoration of Nos. 3 & 5.

Church Street, North West side and St. James' Close

35 St. James Church's records date from 1538. The present building was erected 1819/20. Its vaulted roof is supported by groups of four pine columns brought from Newfoundland by Poole's sailing brigs. It contains many memorials dating from 1608 up to the American flag hanging before the chancel presented by the American forces stationed in Poole as they left for the Normandy invasion. The Union Jack hung opposite is said to be the first flag raised over liberated Paris in 1944.

36 The St James Bell-ringers. This old photograph of St. James bell-ringers could only have been taken in the bell-tower by it being partially enclosed in scenery. In the old days the townspeople were awakened each morning by St. James's 'Rising Bell', rung from the tower at 5.45 each morning except in the four months from November to February when it was rung an hour later.

37 St. James' Close. Nos. 1 & 3 West Street were originally built as a single house but in about 1700 had been divided into two and considerably altered some hundred years later. No. 3 had been refronted. By 1965 their condition precluded restoration. In the reconstruction, West Street was closed at this point and the remaining part renamed St. James' Close.

Church Street – North West side

38 The reredos, St. James Church, made of Spanish mahogany, was given to the old church in 1736 by Richard Pennell. It was taken down during the demolition of the old church and eventually re-erected in the new building. It records the Creed, the Ten Commandments and the Lord's Prayer.

Church Street – South East side

39 'The Saint James Sabbath Schools', 1862. The building was erected in that year to accommodate the Sunday School which had been established in Poole in 1789. At the celebration of its Jubilee 702 children attended the Memorial Service in the church. They were given tea after the service and it was recorded that the children consumed 657lbs of cake (costing £19 3s 3d)! The building was hit by a bomb in the last war and its roof was severely damaged and the building has never regained its original distinction.

41 The entrance of the scrap-yard which took the place of the timber-framed houses.

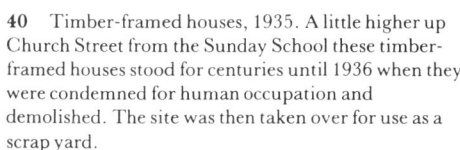

40 Timber-framed houses, 1935. A little higher up Church Street from the Sunday School these timber-framed houses stood for centuries until 1936 when they were condemned for human occupation and demolished. The site was then taken over for use as a scrap yard.

Church Street, Market Street – North West side

Nos 2, 4 & 6   No 8   No 10   No 12   No 14 Church St   Levet's Lane   No 2 Market St   No 4

42 Nos. 2, 4, 6 and 8 Church Street. The owners opted to restore these four houses themselves. The first three houses are taller than most buildings of this character in Poole. No. 2 formerly had a shop window facing the street which had been replaced by a close-set pair of windows. No. 8, built in the early 18th century, had had a shop window added in the 19th century.

43 14 Church Street prior to restoration. A house built in the 18th century which had had its central window above the front door blocked in. 'Blake House' lay behind it facing Levet's Lane which ran beside No. 14 and led round the garden of the Rectory and past the Dolphin Brewery to enter West Street between 'Poplar House' and the Mineral Water Works.

44 10-14 Church Street after restoration. No. 10 was originally built as a single house in the late 16th century. It was later refronted in brickwork and converted into a pair of cottages which became Nos. 10 and 12 Church Street. When the building was restored it was converted back into a single house.

Market Street, Church Street – South-East Side

No 7   No 5   No 3   No 1   St George's Almshouses   Cinnamon Lane   31 Church St

45 Cinnamon Lane runs off to the right between the Almshouses and Blenheim House. The Almshouses were originally built to house the four priests serving the four altars of the original St. James's Church, – the High Altar, the Lady Altar, St. Catherine's Altar and the Altar of St. George.

The Corporation bought the building in 1586 and converted it into Almshouses and administered them until they were transferred to the Board of Governors of the Poole Union under the Poor Law Amendment Act of 1834.

Market Street – North West side

No 10   No 12   No 14 Church St   Levet's Lane   No 2 Market St   No 4   No 6   No 8   No 10   No 12

46 Church Street ends at Levets Lane and Market Street leads north from the other side of the lane. No. 2 Market Street was built in the early 1600's and later had its front room and front door replaced by a modern shop front. No. 4 was built a little later to fill in the space between No. 2 and 6. No. 6 and No. 8 Market Street were originally one house built of stone and timber and divided into two in the mid-1700's. Nos. 10 and 12, built in 1762, were also originally a single dwelling. The wooden gates further up the road formed the entrance to Wessex Industries, fork-lift manufacturers.

47 No. 2 Market Street, the shop, was found to be incapable of restoration. It was demolished and a house, designed to conform with the buildings of the Precinct, was built on the site.

Market Street – South East side

The Yacht Inn   New Street   No 13   No 11   No 9   No 7   No 5   No 3
                                                                                                          Market Street

48 Nos. 13 – 5 Market Street before restoration. Nos. 13 & 11 were formerly one dwelling. No. 13 was built in 1722 and No. 11 in the early 1800's as an annexe to it with internal access only. When the house was divided a doorway was inserted in the place of a window. No. 9, Bowden House, was built in the mid-18th century with a wide frontage to the street but only one room in thickness and without any window openings in the rear wall. The kitchen was added to the back of the house in the 19th century. Nos. 5 & 7 were built in the mid-18th century as a single house and divided into two in the early 19th century.

49 Nos. 7 – 13 Market Street while the restoration of Nos. 11 & 13 was proceeding.

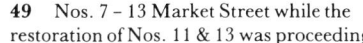

50 Nos. 13 – 5 Market Street after restoration. No. 13 was returned to its original appearance. The roof timbers were replaced and felted and the original stone slates were then put back. The Yacht Inn was later reconstructed to become The Guildhall Tavern.

New Street   North-West Side

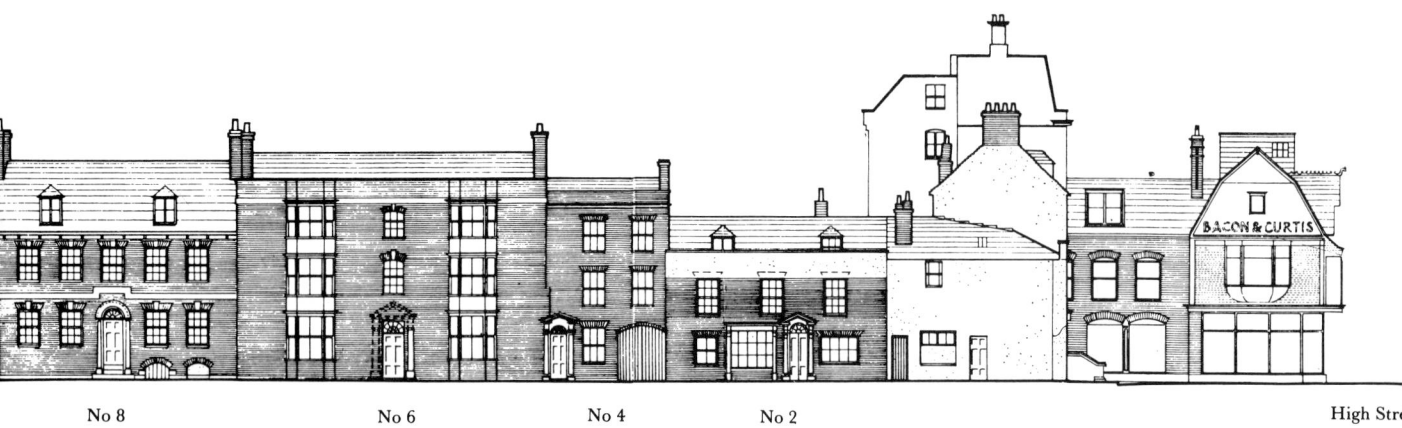

No 8   No 6   No 4   No 2   High Stre(Corn Mar

51 When the Georgian Society were consulted about the Corporation's proposals for the redevelopment of Old Poole and the establishment of the Precinct its main suggestion was that the buildings on the north side of New Street should also be preserved if this was possible. It was, however, finally decided to be impossible. This photograph is of New Street in 1958.

52 Cinnamon Lane led into New Street at the side of the old Ostler's premises. New Street itself led from High Street into Market Street opposite the entrance to Wessex Industries in Market Street. Nos. 6 & 8 New Street were the only Poole mansion houses incapable of rehabilitation.

53 No. 2 New Street in 1962 had been redecorated to form a Craft shop by Audrey Crew. Up to 1957 it had been the premises of the Baverstock's who for many years had baked bread in the stone ovens for sale on the premises. The original building had been erected in the 1600's but had been refronted in the late 1700's.

Market Street   North-West Side

| No 18 | No 20 | No 22 | No 24 | No 26 | The Angel | The Old Greyhound Inn | King Street | The Wellington Inn No 34 |

54 Wellington House, 1958. At this time Market Street ran on past the Guildhall to join Hunger Hill. When the new lateral road, New Orchard, was built just north of the Guildhall and cutting Market Street into two, the northern half of Market Street was renamed Market Close. The plaque in the window of Wellington House commemorated the fact that Thomas Bell FRGS had been born in the house in 1792. The house had later been converted into the Duke of Wellington public House and later, after being used for some time as a shop, had reverted to use as a private house.

55 The Old Greyhound Inn, Market Street, was built in 1770. The Inn had later been divided when two of the ground floor windows on either side of the original entrance were replaced by shop windows and a separate shop had been formed of this part of the inn.

On this side of King Street and just before it reached Roger's Almshouses in West Street (photo 192) was the old Corporation's Yard and Depot and the Town Gaol. On the opposite side of the street had been the offices of Poole's own Court of Record.

56 No. 1 King Street – 34 Market Street (Wellington House). King Street was known as Market Lane in the 18th century.

The Guildhall

57 When the Corporation elected Joseph Gulston and Lt/Col Thomas Calcraft to Parliament in 1761 they each promised to give £750 to the Corporation to build a Market House. The Corporation added a Council chamber above the market to replace its old Council chamber above the prison in Fish Street (later Castle Street). The market had open-fronted shops and comprised the town's Meat Market. The Corporation already had its Fish Market on the Quay and a 'Green Market' and Butter Market nearby.

58 Robert Pearce, one of the macebearers, 1930.

59 Messrs Reid & Paytress, macebearers, 1950. The two large maces were given to the Corporation in 1780 by Morton Pitt, then one of Poole's two MP's. The appointment of two sergeants-at-mace was authorised in 1568 by Queen Elizabeth's Charter.

G. B. BILLOWS,

WHOLESALE AND RETAIL
IRONMONGER;

Brazier, Tin-plate Worker, Cutler, Bell Hanger; Gun, Lock, Copper, and White Smith,

HIGH STREET, POOLE,

Most respectfully informs his friends and the public that he Manufactures every description of Register, Half-register, Eliptic, Rumford, Laundry, Ship, Hall, and other STOVES, Kitchen RANGES upon improved principles with Ovens, Boilers, &c. Also, every article in the TIN and COPPER BRANCHES, a large assortment of which, with a very extensive Stock of ...ERY, CUTLERY, &c., he has CONSTANTLY ON SALE

Factory and Ware Rooms:

CONSISTING OF
common Fire Irons, Br...
and pressed F...

FOR THE BEST PHONOGRAPHS and RECORDS
(GENUINE EDISON'S),
GO TO
CHAS. F. SMITH'S,
Pianoforte and Music Stores,
HANDEL HOUSE,
HIGH STREET, POOLE

Edison's 'Gem' Phonograph, .. £2 2s.
Edison's 'Standard' Do., .. £4 4s.
Edison's 'Home' Do., .. £6 ..

Bacon & Curtis, Ltd.,
44 & 180, HIGH ST., POOLE.

IRONMONGERS & ENGINEERS.

Specialities:—
...ighting and Hot Water Engineering.
... AT STORE PRICES.

...TED OLD HOUSE FOR
Wines and Spirits.

All well known brands kept in stock.

...ENT FOR
Groves & Sons'
Weymouth
Ales.

WHITE HART HOTEL
(4 DOORS FROM POST OFFICE)
HIGH ST., POOLE.

H. J. BURCH, PROPRIETOR.

A FAST, WELL FOUND 10 TON YACHT FOR HIRE.

Herbert Saunders

Wholesale & Family Grocer,

BREAD, CAKE, AND ....
SHIP BISCUIT MANUFACTURER,

93, HIGH STREET, POOLE.

TELEPHONE No. 8X.

High Street

Surprisingly, the properties in High Street were first numbered from north to south, starting at Ivy House on the corner of South Street. It was therefore necessary when High Street was extended into Longfleet to renumber the properties and it was then numbered upwards from the Quay.

Then, having been extended into Longfleet, High Street became the main traffic route through the Old Town in lieu of Towngate Street and, though it was only 16 feet wide in places, it remained so until the 1960's.

Long before this the road had become a serious bottleneck for traffic and was made worse by the fact that the only reasonable cross-road between West Quay Road, West Street, High Street and Lagland Street was the Quay itself. An early proposal to improve the route from the bridge to High Street is shown on the 1841 plan of Poole reprinted as end-papers to this book. It even got as far as being given a name, but no one seems to have seriously contemplated changing High Street as the main north-south highway.

The railway crossing the top end of High Street with its level crossing exacerbated the congestion. In the last war, with most civilians dependant for their travel on the buses, and with the railway traffic increased by the demands of the war, the disruption of the bus time-tables became serious enough for the Corporation to build a new road, Kingland Crescent, over the end of the Ladies Walking Field so that the bus terminus could be transferred to it from Library Corner near South Street to avoid the level crossing.

At the same time the Corporation became very concerned over the congestion of High Street itself and when the Fifty-Shilling Tailor's shop in High Street was bombed the Corporation tried to persuade the owners to set back the new building to allow land for the widening of High Street. The Council were unsuccessful so, to be able to compel owners to set back their buildings on any future rebuilding, it prescribed a new building line for High Street. The new line ensured that, even if only one side of the road was redeveloped it would be at least 40 feet wide throughout. It was a popular decision. 'People had long ago given up all hope of ever seeing the antiquated thoroughfare being improved,' wrote the local newspaper. 'The Council's move to a better High Street will please everybody,' it reported.

The following year the Council's Building and Town Planning Committee developed the idea further. It decided that the Quay should be widened to provide an adequate connecting road and that West Quay Road and Lagland Street should be widened.

These proposals needed the confirmation of the Ministry of War Transport. After holding an inquiry the Ministry decided that the Council's proposals offered no satisfactory long-term solution. It decided that this could only be achieved by a new road being built runing south-north from the bridge through the town with a new bridge built over the railway and that the other proposals of the Council should await the redevelopment of Poole after the war.

The Corporation's proposed new building line for High Street was therefore never confirmed. The only effect it had was in the compromise which had meanwhile been reached with Woolworth's store when the main building was built to the proposed new building line but the ground floor was allowed to be extended to the old building line.

In the redevelopment of Old Poole in the 1960's a new road was constructed between the Bridge and Longfleet and, instead of widening the Quay, a new cross-road, New Orchard, was built connecting Lagland Street, High Street and West Quay Road. Which allowed High Street and its buildings to remain substantially as they were.

60 Poole's first library, a subscription library, was never successful. It was closed on the completion of the free public library in South Street and was occupied by the Cornelia Working Men's Club. After the war for some years it was occupied by the Missions to Seamen and later used as a youth club. In 1963 it was bought by the Poole Harbour Commissioners and demolished for their new offices to be built on the site.

61 The lower end of High Street at the turn of the century. Two famous Poole Inns are on the left. The King's Head was a favourite haunt of the old Poole sea captains whose habit was to sign their names on the glass of the panelled door leading from the bar. The Antelope was the scene of much of Poole's old history. It then still boasted its antelope and flag pole. Both inns were built in the 16th century and remodelled in the 18th. The Antelope originally had mansard attics but was heightened to three stories in the 19th century.

62 14 – 22 High Street in 1874. No. 14, the first shop on the left was built in the 16th century as a single house with No. 12. It has a fine Tudor ceiling to its upstairs room. The Star Hotel was then on the opposite side of the road.

63 A later photograph of the north-west side of High Street showing The King's Head Inn rebuilt with dormer windows inserted in the roof. On the right are the warehouses of Belben's Mill which was on the Quay.

64 On the south east side of High Street, just above the Antelope. Nos. 21 – 27 High Street lay between Dennetts Lane, leading off to the Strand and Bell Lane which led into Castle Street. The buildings were erected in the 16th century and were then occupied either as a whole or in two pairs. When Nos. 23 & 25 were demolished in 1962 stone walls of an earlier 15th century building were revealed. On the immediate right of the photograph the door shown leads to the living quarters of Mr. Adolphus Shutler's shop where for many years he provided sailors' clothing.

High Street – West side

65 The Corn Market seen from Fish (Castle) Street, 1873. Market stands were erected in the small square when it was used as the town corn market. New Street leads off to the left. George Norton's ironmongery and stationer's shop was then numbered 132 High Street. Walter Bacon bought the business in the early 1880's.

66 The same view some thirty years later. Mr. Bacon had rebuilt George Norton's shop. He had been appointed supplier to the Prince of Wales and opened branch shops at Parkstone, Westbourne and Bournemouth. His son joined the firm and it became Bacon & Curtis. There was a plaque on the wall of the building which read: *KING CHARLES II and the unfortunate Duke of Monmouth dined at the House formerly standing on this site 15th September, 1665.* This building was demolished in recent years for the erection of an office block, Latimer House.

67 78 – 88 High Street. The much-photographed thatched cottage in High Street was one of the very few thatched houses in Poole. The very narrow streets made thatch too great a fire hazard. No. 80 was Thomas Atkin's house and chemist's shop. The Minerva Printing Works next door became Looker's stationery shop. The building further up the street with the flagpole was the London Inn.

68 78/80 High Street. The thatched cottage was demolished in 1919 and the first Woolworth's store in Poole was built on its site and over part of Mr Atkin's living quarters.

69 A little further up the street New Orchard ran west from High Street to Market Street at a point nearly opposite the Angel. New Orchard was closed in the reconstruction of Old Poole and its name was transferred to the new cross-road which was built from Lagland Street to West Quay Road and which incorporated the old Bowling Green Alley which had run from High Street to Market Place north of the Guildhall.

70   The junction of High Street, Towngate Street & Hill Street in 1872. The premises shown on the right of this photograph were soon to house the Amity Hall in its back garden. The odd shop was then beginning to appear in this part of High Street.

71   The Bull's Head Inn, 1869. The Bull's Head Inn is shown on the immediate left. It was built in the early 1700's. The long sign above the shop two doors further down the street advertises George Wareham's corn and flour stores. The people outside the Bull's Head were probably waiting for the 'Beaminster Omnibus' which ran from this spot at 8.30 and 12.30 each day to Bournemouth. A few years later the railway had ruined most of these horse-drawn services.

72 Weston House was built by the Weston family about 1750 in a little lane off the eastern side of High Street and which became known as Weston's Lane. A further house was built at the side of it and named The Hermitage. Weston House was used as Poole's first hospital but, by 1960, both houses had become derelict after years of use as tenements.

73 The entrance gates to Weston House with the Jolliffe family's emblem of eagle heads on the gate piers. The columns have now been erected at the entrance drive of the Jolliffe's house near Salisbury.

74 St. Paul's Church. In the early 1800's there was considerable public concern at the lack of church accommodation in Poole. By the 1830's handbills were circulating in the town calling for the erection of a church of ease to reduce the congestion at St. James. The handbills pointed out that Poole's population then approached 10,000 with the adjoining parishes of Longfleet and Parkstone, and yet St. James provided accommodation for a mere 1,800. St. Pauls was built on the west side of High Street opposite Globe Lane.

75 St. Paul's Chancel and Nave from Chapel Lane. In 1880 the Chancel and north-west end of the nave was rebuilt in Gothic style. The Amity Lodge of Freemasons sponsored the building and Mr. Montague Guest, Lord Wimborne's brother, who was then Worshipful Master, and his mother, Lady Charlotte Shreiber, laid commemorative tablets in the foundations. In 1960 it was decided that St. Paul's was no longer required and it was demolished in 1963 and its site sold for the erection of shops. £25,000 of the sale price went to refurbish St. James and the window on the south side of St. James showing the Crucifixtion came from the east window of St. Paul's.

76 The Amity Hall, 1890. 127 High Street was built about 1766 as a mansion house for James Olive. It was bought by the Garland family in 1783. In 1850 it was extended at the back and, in 1882, a large hall was built in the back garden which was used by the Amity Lodge of Freemasons and became known as Amity Hall. It was later converted into a cinema. The building adjoining was the 'Piano and Music Warehouse' and, further on, was the Globe Hotel.

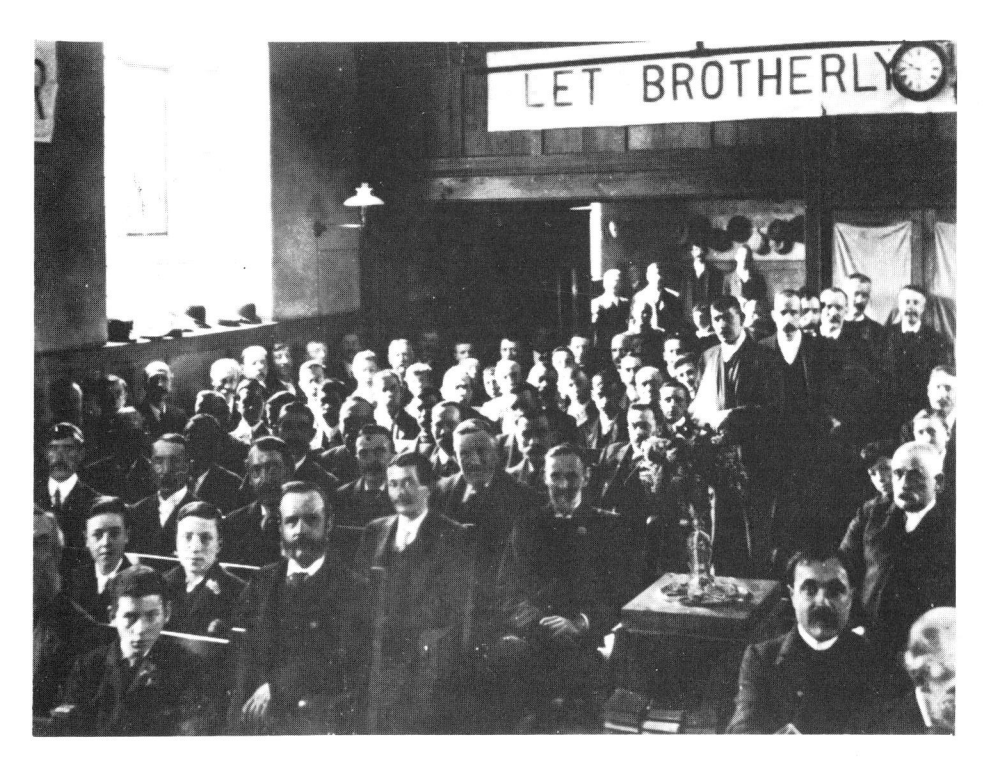

77, 78 The Amity Hall was used for many years as the main place for public gatherings. These photographs show the inaugural meeting in 1906 which led to the formation of the Poole Adult School. Afterwards the school was held every Sunday morning at 9 am at the Friends Meeting House in Lagland Street. It was a very successful venture: it required two of Kinson Pottery's steam engine to pull trucks containing over 200 men and their wives to their Annual Outing a few years later. The school continued until the 1930's.

79 Looking down High Street in 1870. Ivy House, the home of the Penney's is on the left. North Street lies to the right. Few shops have yet appeared in this part of High Street and the Weslyan Chapel had yet to be built. The large building adjoining Ivy House was a terrace of four houses built in 1819 with their kitchen in the basement and whose ground floors were later converted into shops.

80 The railway gates were not too serious an inconvenience in the early part of the century with horse traffic and hand-drawn bath chairs.

81 The top end of High Street, 1870. Beech Hurst, the mansion house to the right, was known as 'White's Place' at the time of the photograph. The Whites were Quakers and therefore took no part in the government of the town but were powerful merchants in the Newfoundland trade. The mansion was built by Samuel Rolles, whose arms are above the building, in 1798 after marrying Dove White. Her daughter, Dove Steele, inherited the property but later it was variously used, first as a private school, then a furniture shop and, more recently, as professional offices.

82 The bottom end of High Street, c1860. Providence Street (later called Paradise Street) led to the right at the side of the library. Its open arcades were blocked-in in 1867.

Poole Park and its Royal Opening

Poole Council had often discussed the need for a 'Peoples' Park', but it was not until 1885 that it finally resolved to provide one. Then, as any land for such a park would inevitably have to come from the lord of the manor, a deputation was appointed to wait upon Lord Wimborne. The generous Lord of the manor, however, needed no persuading that the people of Poole needed a park. He replied that if the Council undertook to convert the land into a park he would be pleased to give them the 26 acres of land which surrounded the backwaters of Parkstone Bay which had been cut off by the railway from Poole to Parkstone.

The land was not then in too salubrious a state. It required considerable in-filling and levelling, and the deep drainage channels round the edges of the bay presented problems, but it was ideally situate between Old Poole, Longfleet and Parkstone. The Poole Council gratefully accepted his offer.

83 H.R.H. The Prince of Wales.

84 H.R.H. The Princess of Wales.

When John Elford, the Borough Surveyor, and Edmund Van Schepdael, his newly-appointed Dutch Surveyor, were given the problem of designing the proposed part they felt it was necessary to add a further 14 acres to Lord Wimborne's land to produce a satisfactory park, and persuaded the Council to acquire this extra land. A few years later the extra land had been acquired, the plans for the construction of the new park had been agreed and a firm of landscape gardeners from Exeter were already well ahead with the work when the Mayor of Poole received a letter from Lord Wimborne. Edward, Prince of Wales, with Princess Alexandra and their children were to visit Canford for a few days during the following January, he told the Mayor, and he felt certain that the Prince would be glad to open the new park if the Corporation were formally to ask him to do so.

The members of the Council were delighted at the thought of a royal opening for their park and, as soon as they had obtained confirmation from the Prince, the Sheriff (Christopher Hill Junr) called a public meeting to form a Committee to organise the event and to raise funds for it. The Mayor started the fund with a donation of £30 and it was decided that a large Pavilion should be erected in the park for the ceremony and that tickets to attend the ceremonies would be put on sale. The great day was to be 17 January, 1890, the last day of the Prince's visit to Canford. The ceremonies would consist of a drive by the Prince and his entourage starting at the borough boundary at Sea View. He would drive through Parkstone to the pavilion in the park for the main ceremonies. He would then drive through the streets of Old Poole before returning to the railway station where he would board the royal train at 1.30 pm for his return journey to London.

That January, however, happened to be the time when influenza, said to have come from Siberia, swept through the country and the Prince's visit, to quote a contemporary report, 'was deprived of part of its agreeable accompaniment' by the sudden absence of the Princess of Wales who, with her daughters Victoria and Maud, were 'afflicted with severe colds'. Moreover, the contagion had already reached Canford where Lord Wimborne himself had retired to bed with the usual fever and aches and pains and had been ordered to stay there.

However, the Prince and his son, Prince George, with Prince Hohenlohe, the Governer of Alsace Lorraine, duly arrived at Wimborne Station on the evening of Wednesday, 14 January, to be met by Ivor and Montagu Guest, two of Lord Wimborne's sons, with their carriage-and-four. The station had been 'tastefully decorated and illuminated' and, it was reported, a crowd of some hundred people 'raised a cheer' as the royal train drew in and, in the square in front of the station, the Wimborne Volunteers and a detachment of the Dorset (Queen's Own) Yeomanry did the honours as the Prince and his party came from the station.

At Canford all had been done to make the Princes' stay enjoyable. There was good shooting, it was said, in the Canford covers. Lord Wimborne had had a billiard room added to the house a year or so earlier, and many friends of the Prince and Lady Wimborne had been invited as house guests during the Prince's stay. They included the Marquis and Marchioness of Ormonde, Sir Edward and Lady Guinness, Sir E Edwards, Viscount and Viscountess Curzon, Lady Romsey, Lady F Marsham, Lord and Lady Randolph Churchill, Earl and Countess Yarborough, Countess Dudley, Lord and Lady Gosford, Lady Sarah Churchill, Viscount Valletort, Mr Harvey, Lord Chelsea, Lord Clifden, Earl Shaftesbury, Lord F Clinton Hope and Mr Alfred Montgomery.

The Prince, however, had little time to enjoy the shooting or billiards at Canford. The day after his arrival he had a full day of engagements in Bournemouth. Accompanied by Lady Wimborne, Lady Yarborough and Lady Romsey, he first went to the marquee erected in the Bournemouth pleasure grounds to receive the loyal addresses of the Bournemouth Improvement Commissioners and the local masonic lodges. Then followed the reception given by the Christchurch Corporation at the Royal Bath Hotel to meet the Mayors of the boroughs of Hampshire, Dorset and Wiltshire. He had then broken off for lunch at Branksome Dene, a villa owned by Lord Wimborne, before undertaking the formal opening of the Victoria Hospital, Bournemouth's memorial to Queen Victoria's Jubilee. He had then completed his afternoon's duties with a visit to St Peter's Church and the Cairns Memorial Home before returning to Canford House to prepare for the banquet at the Royal Bath Hotel given by the Bournemouth Commissioners.

The weather had been bright and fine and the Bournemouth proceedings had all gone smoothly. The flamboyant Mr Budge, the Mayor of Poole, had been the guest of Bournemouth throughout the day and, with the Poole Council having provided themselves and their officers with new robes for the occasion, he and his two splendidly dressed Sergeants-at-Mace had made quite a stir. Mr Budge must, however, have felt confident that Poole could emulate Bournemouth in the opening of the park on the Saturday for enough money had been raised to make the occasion a really splendid one. The streets all the way from Parkstone Park to Poole Park as well as all the streets of Old Poole through which the Prince was to drive had been lavishly decorated. Splendid triumphal arches had been built in Lower Parkstone and in High Street. A large marquee or Pavilion had been erected in the park for the ceremonies and just in front of it there was the imposing, life-size model of the old town wall and gates of Poole through which the Prince and his entourage were to drive. A band had been hired to play in the Pavilion for the ceremonies. The Mayor must have been quite confident that all had been done to make the Prince's visit most memorable.

The Prince had no formal engagements on the following day other than Lady Cornelia's Reception in the evening at Canford House. All the local dignitaries had been invited as well as the Commanding Officers of the Army and Navy detachments involved in the following day's proceedings. The Reception formed a most suitable climax to the Prince's stay at Canford which had been so successful and so blessed with ideal weather.

But, even as the Reception at Canford House was coming to an end, the Fates changed sides. As the Mayor of Poole and his companions left Canford House at 3 am the following morning they found that a storm was raging. As the horses of their carriage stumbled back to Poole through the blackened countryside the storm intensified. Hurrican gusts of wind drove the heavy downpour in swathes of blinding rain against the windows of the carriage as the horses lurched their burden back to Poole.

The storm continued all that night. It was not until 8 o'clock, as daylight broke over Poole, that it abated. It left its rearguard of clouds scudding across a bright sky and showing only too clearly the extent of the damage it had inflicted. The Corporation's lavish preparations for the main ceremony in the park was utterly ruined. The Mayor and his officers needed only a glance at the wreckage of the Pavilion to know that there was not the slightest hope of the ceremonies taking place in it that day. The only crumbs of comfort for the Mayor was that the two triumphal arches, protected by their adjoining buildings, had survived and there was, perhaps, time to put the street decorations back into some sort of order.

To quote a contemporary report, 'the Mayor put himself into prompt communication with Canford Manor to notify them of the disaster'. There was no possible alternative venue for the ceremonies. It was finally and reluctantly agreed that there was no alternative but to delay the Prince's arrival in Poole, for him and his cavalcade to make their promised tour of the town, and then for him formally to declare the park open in a ceremony to be arranged on the platform of the railway station before he boarded his train. It was a very disappointing second-best, but it was the best that could be thought of.

It was therefore not until 12.30 that the Dorset Yeomanry Hussars, resplendent in their dress uniform and with drawn swords, led the royal cortege of vehicles up to Sea View with the Prince of Wales, Lady Cornelia Wimborne, Prince George and Prince Hohenlohe in the first carriage, followed by the other guests from Canford House in carriages behind.

Despite their long wait the 'motley crowd of farmers, peasants and sailors' (to quote the *Daily Telegraph*) gave the Prince a vociferous welcome. His carriage drew up before the assembled members of the Council for the Mayor formally to welcome the Prince to the borough. The Mayor then took his place in the grand carriage with postilions with which he had provided himself. His two Sergeants-at-Mace climbed into the box seats, and the Mayor led the procession off on its journey through the town.

As the column moved off, scores of 'traps' of all kinds, from phaetons to dog-carts, fell in behind; youngsters ran shouting after the carriages and others chased over the heath to meet the column as it came down Springfield Road. The scene was said to be more reminiscent of a

Meet of Foxhounds in a holiday period rather than the start of a State drive.

The Prince had been given a most friendly and boisterous first welcome to Poole. It was, too, the same noisy, cheerful reception which he received throughout his journey through the town. School children lined up along Parkstone Park added their shrill and prolonged welcome to the Prince as his carriage turned into Commercial Road as he came upon the colourful decorations of Parkstone. High 'Venetion Masts', coloured a brilliant red, had been erected on each side of the road and long lines of bunting had been crossed and recrossed between them to give a most festive air to the little village and, not content with this, an 'Alexandra Arch' had been built between the houses on each side of the road near Ashley Cross. It was a high archway through which the Prince would drive, decorated with greenery and covered with loyal inscriptions round a central motif of welcome to the absent Princess of Wales.

It is doubtful whether the Prince of Wales would have had time to read many of the inscriptions on Alexandra Arch for the Mayor led the carriages at a brisk pace. They were soon down Sloop Hill and entering the park at 'Holly Bank'. Once inside, they were soon upon the centre-piece of the town's decorations which seems to have been put into position in time for the Prince's arrival. It was an enormous replica of Poole's old Town Wall with two mock-stone gateways across the two carriageways of the new park. The imitation ramparts had been decorated with armorial bearings and standards and, in large letters across the whole face of it, had been painted 'Welcome to our Ancient Borough'. Then, to add verisimilitude, even the shape of the old town houses lying beyond the wall had been depicted.

The original plan was that as soon as the Prince had passed through the mock Town Gates he would come upon the Mayor standing outside the Pavilion, flanked by his two Sergeants-at-Mace, waiting to receive the Prince and his party and lead them to their seats of honour in the great marquee where the Bournemouth Silver Band had been installed ready to strike up with the National Anthem.

But that morning, as the Mayor led the carriages through the mock gateway, they immediately came upon the dismal sight of what had been the Mayor's proud Pavilion. It lay prostrate, a mass of sodden canvas, heaving slightly in the wind over the wreckage of its stage and seating.

Happily, though, it was soon behind them and the Prince had other things to take his attention. Another high imitation stone archway had been built across High Street near Chapel Lane, and a great mass of flags and bunting almost roofed-in the narrow High Street. Then there was the Antelope Hotel where the Prince had stayed with his tutor overy thirty years earlier. Then, on the corner of the Quay there was the Poole lifeboat which had been hauled up on to the Quay, with the Crew in full dress of sou'westers and cork lifebelts, standing to attention in it. As he turned along the Quay there was the impressive sight of the crews manning the yard arms of their ships moored at the Quay and, when they turned up Thames Street they were greeted by a 'glorious peal' of bells from St. James. They were then on the last lap of their drive in West Street. The little orphan girls, lined up outside Dorset House in their best little dresses and pinafores, sang 'God Bless the Prince of Wales' as they passed on the last lap of their tour of the borough.

Poole had given the Prince of Wales, his son and their friends a right royal welcome. The revised programme had gone well and the weather had remained fine. But it was not the Mayor's lucky day for another trial awaited him at the railway station.

The Princes' safety, once he set foot on railway property, became the responsibility of the railway police. In the hurried rearrangements the railway police had not been consulted and, as he entered the railway station, the Mayor was told that the railway police had decreed that any ceremonies in which the Prince of Wales was to participate could not take place on the open platform of the station. If any ceremony was to take place on railway property it had to be indoors – and the only place they could suggest was the railway booking office!

The Prince of Wales was not far behind the Mayor. There was not time to argue the point. The Mayor had no alternative but to accept the position and to put as brave a face as possible on it. He welcomed the Prince as he arrived at the booking office with Lady Cornelia and the Princes and explained the need for yet another change of programme. He then presented the Sheriff and Town Clerk and asked the Prince to accept an illuminated address of loyalty from the town. The Prince of Wales accepted the address and, as there was clearly no point in them reading their prepared speeches to each other in the privacy of the little booking office, the Prince handed to the Mayor the text of his intended speech on opening the park (in which, it was later found, that the Prince expressed himself 'deeply interested in the important question of providing open-air spaces for the inhabitants of towns' and saying that it gave him 'the greatest satisfaction in opening the park and recreation ground.') Lady Cornelia then presented the Prince with a bouquet of orchids which she asked the Prince to give to the sick Princess of Wales – and the proceedings were over. Poole had had its unique and royal opening of its Park!

The royal party then went on to the station platform where the members of the council, the magistrates and other notable guests had been carefully arranged for the proposed ceremonies. They must have been amazed to see the Prince and his entourage already saying their goodbyes as they came from the booking office to board the royal train. The Handel String Band, hurriedly recruited to play on the station platform, were taken utterly by surprise when they were suddenly called upon to play and they struck up in a complete and tuneless confusion.

It must have been, therefore, with considerable relief a few minutes later, that the Mayor saw the royal train drawing out of the station with the Prince of Wales at the open window waving goodbye to his hosts.

Half-an-hour later, those who remained in Poole could relax (except perhaps for the Earl of Shaftesbury and Ivor Guest, both of whom were to make their maiden speeches) as the Corporation gave a luncheon in their newly-decorated Guildhall in honour of Lady Cornelia. And it was to her that Philip Budge, the Mayor, gave the major share of the credit for Poole having at last achieved its park. But officers of the Corporation were also praised, especially John Elford and his surveyor, Edmund van Schepdael, who had designed the park, skilfully incorporating the 50-odd acres of water from the cut-off Parkstone Bay.

The praise was only their due for the park has changed little from its basic design of 1888. For nearly one hundred years many thousands of people each year have enjoyed its amenities while long ago the traumas of its royal opening were forgotten.

85

BOROUGH OF POOLE.

VISIT OF THEIR ROYAL HIGHNESSES

PRINCE & PRINCESS OF WALES

ON 18th INSTANT

TICKETS OF ADMISSION

to the Pavilion to witness the Ceremony of Opening the Peoples' Park by His Royal Highness the Prince of Wales, may be obtained of Messrs. Mate & Sons, Poole and Bournemouth; and Mr. C. J. Woodford, Poole.

PRICES: 7s. 6d., 5s., & 2s. 6d.

Early application is necessary as the number of Seats are limited.

H. SALTER DICKINSON,
TOWN CLERK.

Dated 13th January, 1890.

THE "OLD TOWN WALL," POOLE.

Mr. P. E. L. Budge,
(Mayor of Poole).

91 The Salt Water Lake, the part of Parkstone Bay cut off by the railway line from Poole to Parkstone. It was made an almost uniform depth of 3 feet which made it ideal for pleasure boating. The photograph, taken around 1900, shows development spreading over Lower Parkstone.

92 The carriageway and footpaths of the Park early this century.

93 This early view of Poole Park shows the Bandstand in its original position and the sapling trees just beginning to grow.

94 At the time of this photograph, taken in 1950, the only wildfowl in the park lakes were these mute swans, Muscovy Ducks, coots and militant moorhens. The trees had matured, some of them had even passed their prime.

95 The Dorset Wildfowlers introduced Canada Geese into the park in 1957. Mr. E Bedingfield launched the first goose into the freshwater lake. Later other types of waterfowl were introduced including Mandarins, Carolina ducks, Tufted ducks, Ruddy Sheldrake, Common Sheldrake, Red Crested Pochards, Rosybills, the Common Shoveller and Black Swans, but none have prospered like the Canada Geese which have almost overwhelmed the rest.

96 Poole Park in snow in 1951.

97 Another study by Mr E H P Bristowe of snow in Poole Park in 1951.

98 The War Memorial. It took until 1927 for Poole to erect a monument to the men and women of the town who had been killed in the 1914 – 1818 War. It was too late to ask Edward, Prince of Wales, to unveil it during his visit to the district in October of that year. He did, however, come to Poole after a 'record bustle' of engagements in Bournemouth to lay a wreath at the new memorial where a large crowd had gathered, including most of the school children of the borough, who had been marched there from their schools to witness the short ceremony.

99 Quay View.

The Quay

In Tudor times the Great Quay belied its name for it extended only from the east end of Town Cellars to a point about half way to the site of the present bridge. At the eastern end of Town Cellars a wall was built out towards the Quay enclosing the Great Quay with a large archway leading on to it from High Street. At the eastern side of the wall was a large inlet known as 'Measurer's Gap'.

At this time Poole had only eight ocean-going ships, six of which were employed in the Newfoundland fisheries and two of which traded with Barbados. A hundred years later Poole had 126 ships, most of them ocean-going, and this number increased with the expanding Newfoundland trade in the 18th century until in 1770 Poole had some 250 ships. Even with the addition of Little Quay the lack of quay space was a considerable handicap to trade for ships often had to be moored four and five abreast at the quays. By 1788 Poole's shipping register had risen to 300 and the Corporation were at last forced to try to improve matters. Merchants agreed to give up the open spaces in front of their warehouses so that the quays could be extended eastwards and in 1788 the three quays were realigned to form one long quay. During the following thirty years the Corporation gradually acquired extra pieces of land to improve and lengthen the Quay, frequently hiring a stone mason from Swanage to come to supervise the work.

For all these acquisitions, however, the Quay at the end of the 19th century still only reached a point opposite the end of Lagland Street where the Fish Shambles stood. At this point the Quay ended and the roadway led inland to become East Quay Road. To the harbourside of this road and at the back of the Fish Shambles, was a coal wharf and to the east of this, with a harbour frontage, was Poole Pottery. Further east the harbour bit deeper into the land and here, only reached at high tide, was the Fishermen's Hard where the fishermen used to spread their nets to dry.

It was only in comparatively recent times, in 1893, that the Quay was extended to enclose Poole Pottery and the Fishermen's Hard and, in the redevelopment of Poole in the 1960's the Pottery was extended inland to encompass the site of East Quay Road at the point where it had led inland from the Quay. The Fishermen were allocated an area of the harbour at the end of the extended Quay in compensation for their lost inlet and drying grounds. It was a semi-circular enclosure, protected by wooden piles, later substituted by a bank of Purbeck stone, and had a piece of open land behind it where the fishermen dried their nets.

100

101 The familiar drawing of the Quay from the harbour 'respectfully dedicated to the Merchants, Shipowners and Inhabitants of Poole' in 1833.

102 Poole Quay in about 1900 when it was supported by wooden piles and the highway and railway lines were clearly separated from the Quay.

103 The Great Quay in 1874. The staircase at the side of The Harbour Office led to the Steam Packet Inn, then run by Thomas Harris but, by the following year he had closed it. There was, however, still a choice of six public houses on the Quay as well as Garibaldi Arms and The Coach and Horses in Strand Street, just behind the Quay, to say nothing of the many public houses and inns in the roads leading off the Quay.

104 A 'Coastline' ship at the Quay in 1912. The Coastline Company operated coastal shipping from its offices on the Quay for many years. The old Poole Pottery kilns can be seen at the back of what now appears to be a busy Quay and the Gas Company's coal transporter is in the background. The standard in the middle of the photograph is one of the "Lights in Line" erected to aid navigation of the Main Channel.

105 Poole Quay in 1909. The old wooden piles and the wooden platforms which had previously existed from this point to East Quay were being replaced by a stone quay.

The Ham Ferry

106 Between Quays in 1912. The ferry between the quays had oprated since the 16th century. The Corporation leased the rights to the highest bidder who was then entitled to collect 1d per quarter from each Poole householder and charge strangers ½d per passage. Originally the ferry was operated by a large boat holding 80 people and was pulled across by rope.

107 Later the ferry was operated by two rowing boats. One is here arriving at the Ferry Steps. In 1833, about the time of the controversial building of the first bridge, the ferry rights were put out to tender. To the mortification of the Corporation the lord of the manor, through his new Bridge Company, put in the highest offer. The Corporation refused to complete the licence and the Company successfully sued the Corporation for specific performance. Business fell off after the completion of the bridge and the ferry was finally abandoned after an unsuccessful attempt to revive it in the 1950's.

108 The Shipwright's Arms, Hamside, owned by the Corporation, was built at the side of the Ham Passage House. As the shipbuilding yards were replaced by industrial and commercial premises its business was so reduced that the brewers did not renew the lease and the building was demolished in the 1970's.

109 The large building overlooking the Quay was the large steam-operated mill which was for many years the most prominent building on the Quay and supplied a wide area of the west country. It also had a large warehouse at the bottom of High Street.

110 Fishermen's Depot, 1950. Even now there still are buildings on the Quay reminding Poole of its traditional fishing trades and, at the time of this photograph, dried Newfoundland cod was still on sale in the town.

111 The Fishmarket, 1959. Poole Corporation obtained power by its Charter of 1667 to hold a fish market in the town. It provided that fishermen "taking fish in the fishing places of the town, its liberties and precincts, should bring such fish to the common fishermarket to be exposed for sale for one hour before being carried to any other market or place of sale" Mrs. Kentish, Mayoress of Poole, opened this new fishmarket in May, 1914, after the demolition of the old Shambles. The property had been let on the basis that the fishermen would pay the lessee 6d each time they offered fish for sale there. The fishermen refused to pay more than 2d and usually managed to sell their fish elsewhere. The building became a white elephant, especially when fish catches declined drastically a few years after the 1918 war and the property was let as a store until 1959 when it was demolished.

The Fishermen and their Fleet

112 Pat Matthews, a 'crabber', in 1949.

113 'Curly' Greenslade, 1960, with a 12lb lobster.

114 Henry Matthews in a Poole punt which was originally developed for wildfowling in the shallow waters of the harbour. He is holding the traditional spear which was used by generations of fishermen for eel spearing. In the 1920's several Poole fishermen, headed by 'Chiny' Gould, made a living in supplying the London market with eels.

115 A sprat catch at the Quay. The arrival of sprats in Poole Bay was always problematical. In some winters, usually around Christmas, they arrive in great quantities. In other years hardly any appear. Consequently prices obtained for them vary enormously. In 1935 they were sold for 3d per bushel and Bob Arnold, farmer at Upton, bought the whole catch to plough into his fields as manure. In wartime, a few years later, they were in such great demand that Charles Knott, the Corporation's Weights and Measures Inspector, was appointed 'Sprat Allocation Officer'. The recent 1981/2 winter was another year when sprats came into the Bay in great numbers.

116 The Poole Fishing Fleet, 1910. Poole at this time had about 40 fishing boats. They mainly operated in Poole Bay and caught good quantities of plaice, skate, mackeral and herring. Oyster dredging was already nearly a thing of the past. Soon afterwards petrol-driven boats dredged up huge quantities of fish and destroyed the brood and it became no longer profitable for the Poole fishing boats to continue and fishing became a part-time occupation only.

117 (Inset) The entrance to the fishermen's landing stage, 1913. The fishermen's 'hard' was well back from the harbour waters at low tide.

118 The fishermen's 'Hard' in 1890. The ground used by Poole fishermen for drying their nets 'from time immemorial' on the harbour side of East Quay Road.

119 Fishermen's Dock, 1936. To compensate the fishermen for the loss of their landing stage and drying ground at East Quay a semi-circular enclosure was built out into the harbour at the end of the extended Quay for their use. It is seen in this photograph through the Gas Company's coal transporter which then occupied the site of the present Quay Hotel. The fishing boats still had their sailing rig.

120 The last of the traditional Poole fishing boats, *Polly*, in 1937.

121 'Summer wear for men', at Fishermen's Dock, 1950. Do the men, now around forty years old, recognise themselves?

122 At the lifeboat outlet into Fishermen's Dock, 1950. There is always something of interest for people of all ages on the Quay.

The Quay Railway

123 The Quay in about 1880, when cargoes were still carried by sail, mainly in barrels. Castle Street was still Fish Street and Richard Penney still had his coal business on the corner of Fish Street. The quay railway had not long been laid.

124 The Quay just after the turn of the century. The loop line from Poole station ran through the narrow Nile Row into West Quay Road and then turned to run along the Quay. The shunting of waggons on the Quay lines was banned in the war after a waggon had collided with a Hants & Dorset bus in the black-out. The line was abandoned and the lines removed in 1962.

125 The 'Havre' turning into West Quay Road from the Quay. At this point the train crossed traffic coming from and going to the bridge.

126 'St Malo' on the Quay. There were three engines used for goods traffic between the Quay and the Poole Goods Yard.

The Quay in Wartime

127 The Blockships, 1940. The old merchant ship *Empire Sentinel* and an old warship *HMS Flinders* were stationed in the war at the side of the Main Channel, primed with explosives ready to be sunk to block the channel should any German invasion look like succeeding locally.

128 Temporary Breakwater, New Quay, 1947. In the war a Landing Craft Recovery Unit was based in Poole and many landing craft were left at Poole after the war. A number of them were filled with ballast and sunk to form a breakwater off the Hamworthy quays and served this purpose for many years.

129 Barrage balloons, 1940. A clandestine photograph (private photography was banned in the war) taken from the Quay near the old Fishmarket of barrage balloons flying from ships moored at the Quay. The balloons were flown from ships to deter dive-bombing attacks by the Luftwaffe.

Quayside Types

130 Ship's engineer in mufti, 1952.

131 Quayside worker, 1950.

132 'Finn' Tilsed, Costermonger, 1949.

133 A Poole docker, 1950.

134 Harry Reeves, the Harbour Postman for many years. He set out from the Quay each day in his rowing boat to deliver mail to the islands of the harbour. The Rev Brian Hession made a film called 'Letter to Goathorn' featuring Harry Reeves and his work.

135 Bill Brown and Harry Davis, 1950. Harry Davis was the landlord of the Jolly Sailor on the Quay. He dived off the Quay 37 times to rescue people from drowning and had been awarded the Humane Society's medal for his efforts.

136 Albert Brown and Richard Hayes, 1950. 'Alby' Brown in his spare time played football for Poole Town as well as for the Dorset County team. Richard Hayes, Poole fisherman, was coxswain of the Poole lifeboat for 40 years.

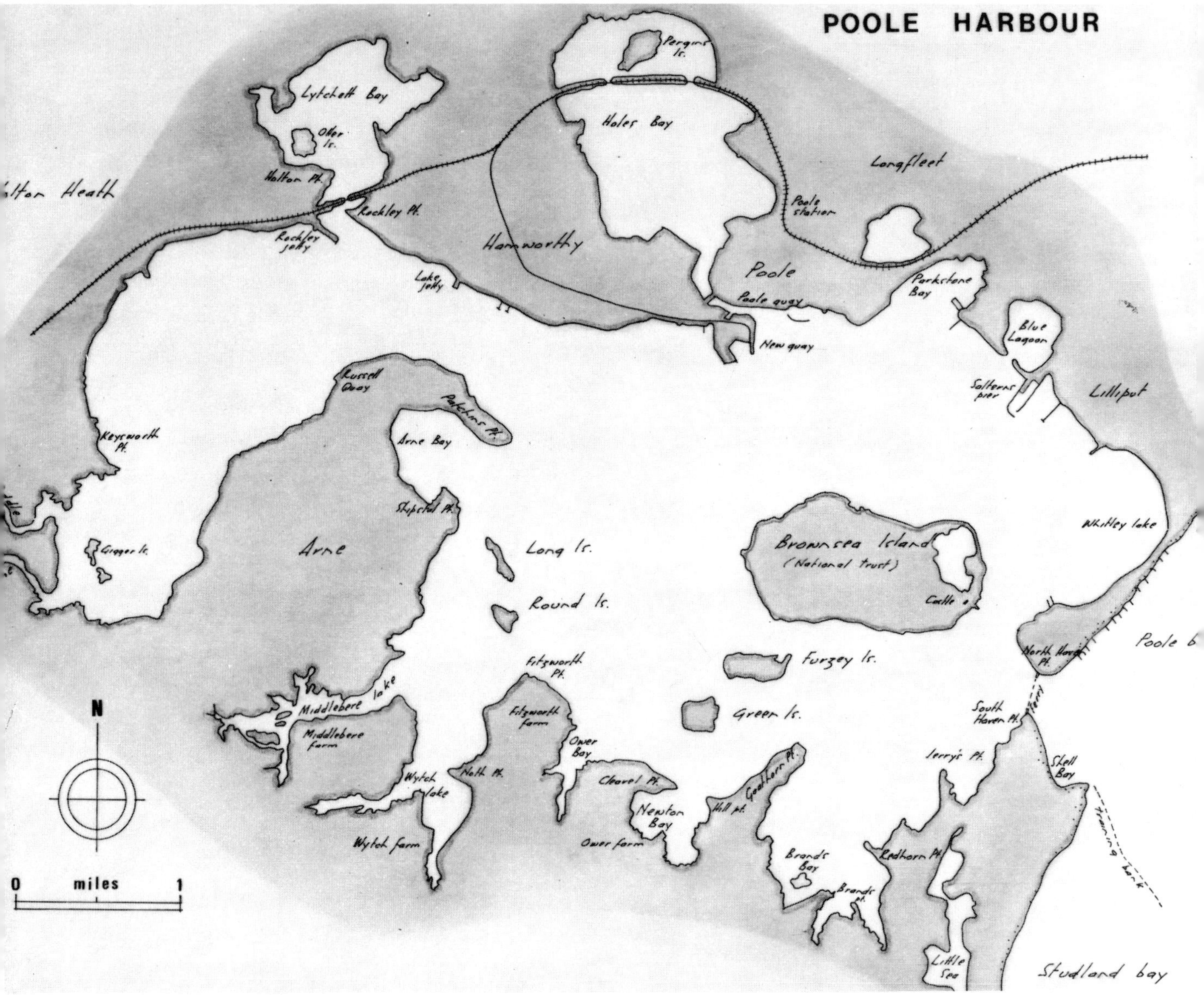
POOLE HARBOUR
Pergins Is.
Lytchett Bay
Otter Is.
Holton Pt.
Holes Bay
Longfleet
Rockley Pt.
Rockley jetty
Poole station
Hamworthy
Poole
Lake jetty
Parkstone Bay
Poole quay
New quay
Blue Lagoon
Russell Quay
Salterns pier
Lilliput
Patchins Pt.
Keysworth Pt.
Arne Bay
Shipstal Pt.
Whitley lake
Brownsea Island
(National trust)
Gigger Is.
Arne
Long Is.
Castle
Round Is.
Poole b
North Haven Pt.
Fitzworth Pt.
Furzey Is.
Middlebere lake
Fitzworth farm
Green Is.
South Haven Pt.
Middlebere farm
Ower Bay
Jerry's Pt.
Shell Bay
Wytch lake
Cleavel Pt.
Goathorn Pt.
Newton Bay
Hill pt.
Wytch farm
Ower farm
Redhorn Pt.
Brands Bay
Brands pt.
N
0 miles 1
Little Sea
Studland bay

137

Poole Harbour

The two long ranges of sandbanks, one running north-east from the Purbeck Hills and the other south-west from the mainland of Poole, restrict the harbour mouth to about 300 yards. Through this small entrance some 36,000,000 tons of water flood into the harbour at ordinary Spring tides. Once inside the harbour the flooding water divides round Brownsea Island. The main thrust is turned north-easterly to form the Main Channel which leads to the Quays over three miles inside the harbour. Once here the tidal flush again divides. Part of it goes on past the Quays to flood Holes Bay, the rest carries on up the Wareham Channel, a further four miles inland, to the marshes lying south of Wareham where, on each side of Giggers Island, the Frome and Piddle Rivers enter the harbour. Meanwhile the subsidiary thrust of the tide through the harbour mouth has been turned south of Brownsea Island to flood round Furzy, Green, Long and Round Islands and the barren shores on the south side of the harbour.

It is, however, only in comparatively recent years that the southern shores of the harbour have been desolate. The little village of Arne was still thriving until it was evacuated compulsorily in the last war so that the Bovington Tank Ranges could be extended. Earlier Wytch was once a clay port. Middlebere was once linked to the Norden clay pits by a light railway and another line linked the clay pits of Godins to the pier at Goathorn. Ower was once the port serving Corfe Castle from which Purbeck stone was first exported. In addition to these activities the southern area of the harbour was heavily shot over by wildflowers, and local men, in search of a change of diet from the usual winter fare of salt pork, regularly stalked duck in their Poole punts along the southern fringes of the harbour. But now the quays, the inns and the light railways as well as the once wide network of roads connecting them with Corfe Castle, Studland and South Haven have all but disappeared and the bare hinterland behind the southern shores of the harbour has been declared an area of outstanding beauty.

One striking feature of the harbour does remain, however, in the double high tide which the harbour has every twelve hours. After the first high water the tide flows out of the harbour for an hour and a half. The tide ebbing out of the harbour mouth then meets the tide flowing strongly along the coast from the Needles. This heavy tide from the east is checked by the headland to the west of Poole and a great quantity of it floods back across the harbour mouth and overwhelms the water leaving the harbour which flows back into the harbour causing a second high tide three hours after the first. The water then stabilizes and the tide makes away for the next three and a half hours to low tide. It then rises for six hours and the process is repeated.

The crucial importance of the harbour to Poole for hundreds of years was that sailing ships could navigate the channels of the harbour and the channel leading from the harbour to the open sea. But, to the consternation of the Merchants, towards the end of the 18th century, it was found that little Channel and Wytch Channel were silting up and, worse still, the 'bar', the bank of sand which the tides formed across the channel leading from the harbour entrance to the open sea, had moved westward and had increased in size and thus had reduced the depth of water above it. They commissioned Robert Whitworth, an engineer, to report on what might be done to remedy the situation. His remedies seemed too drastic and too expensive and nothing was done. Thirty years later, in 1824, they engaged another consulting engineer, James Rendell, to report on what could be done. His report was no more comforting.

He reported that the gradual silting up of harbours not served by great rivers to scour them was inevitable. Silt was brought down into the harbour by the rivers. The harbour was the natural drainage point for the vast areas surrounding Poole Harbour and a great amount of silt and sand was brought into the harbour by the incoming tide which settled as the water lost its momentum. This allowed sandbanks to form and consolidate. The existence of these sandbanks would in their turn reduce the amount of water coming into the harbour. On top of this, Mr Rendell reported, a considerable amount of reclamation of land had taken place on all three sides of Poole which again reduced the quantity of water entering the harbour and therefore the scour of the water returning to the sea at low tide.

His remedy was the same as the earlier expert had advised. Reclamation of land from the harbour should be strictly restricted and Lytchett Bay should be embanked and a canal dug out to join its waters to Holes Bay. The two bays would then form a large reservoir of water which could be impounded by a sluice gate situated between piers built from each side of the Quay. This enormous amount of water could then be let out at an appropriate time near low tide when it would have four times the scouring effect of the ebbing tide and also give a twenty-five per cent increase in the scouring power of the tide over the 'bar' outside the harbour. In 1831 the Council asked him to give them a report on the estimated cost of these works. It came to £14,050.

It was not an opportune time. The Newfoundland trade was in recession and, with the gaining impetus of the Reform Movement, the very existence of the old Corporation was in doubt, a doubt which was translated into a reality four years later when the Municipal Corporations act came into force and then the new Corporation had many other pressing concerns as well as having no resources to allow them to contemplate such an expenditure.

By 1890, however, the new Corporation itself became worried over the silting up of the Quays and the growing obstacle of the 'bar'. By this time only ten feet of water was available over the harbour bar and many ships had to lighten their cargo in the Bay and await high tide before entering the harbour.

The Corporation put out their problem to a competition between engineers to offer solutions to their problem. Mr Kinipple's entry was adjudged the best. He suggested that the Quay should be extended in a straight line to direct the ebbing tide down the main channel, groynes would be erected along the coast at Sandbanks to hold back some of the sand washing down from the east across the harbour entrance (see photo 259) and a groyne built out to sea from the harbour mouth to direct the ebbing tide against the bar to disperse some of the sand which was deposited there. The disputes and Inquiries following the receipt of this report were detailed in our *Album of Old Poole* but the works were completed in the following fifteen years and had considerable beneficial effect on the quay and the harbour entrance, but none of the proposals of the various experts to reduce the silting up of the harbour itself were ever put into effect, apart from some restrictions on reclamation.

Although Mr Rendell's dire warning was probably exaggerated when he wrote that 'if the present evils at work in the estuary are neglected within a few years (the harbour) will to a certain extent undergo the same necessitudes as Wareham', reclamations of land from the harbour and Holes Bay still take place, not least by the Harbour Board itself.

Old Harry Rocks Handfast Point. 187[4]

138 Handfast Point in 1874. Old Harry and his wife, the last two rocks of the promontory of Ballard Down stood sentinel over the entrance to Poole Harbour and welcomed home many generations of Poole mariners.

139 Old Harry rocks in 1910. Old Harry's wife is shrinking but is still visible.

140 Old Harry rocks, 1947. Old Harry is now a widower. His wife has disappeared entirely as well as a great amount of the protecting promontory.

141 South Haven Inn, about 1890. Once at the end of a wide network of roads which connected the little settlements of the Isle of Purbeck. It was used by wildfowlers when shooting duck over the Studland marshes. It was also conveniently placed for mariners held in the harbour by contrary winds as well as for the stone boats of Swanage taking shelter in the harbour. When it was found possible to feed cattle in the winter and when steam-driven ships took over from sailing ships the Inn lost its custom and was eventually abandonned. By the beginning of the First World War only fragments of its foundations remained.

142 Goathorn Pier, 1913. Goathorn, the promontory on the southern shores of the harbour, was the terminus of Fayle & Co's little railway bringing clay from their pits at Godins. Here it was loaded into barges to be transported to ocean-going ships moored at the Quay. Most of the clay was taken to Runcorn, near Liverpool, where it was again manhandled into barges to be taken by canal to Stoke to be made into Staffordshire ware. The pier was destroyed in 1940 as a wartime precaution when the German invasion was threatened.

Some Famous Poole Ships

143 The *Result*, a steel schooner which was built in Belfast in 1893. She became a 'Q' ship in the First World War. Afterwards she was re-rigged to take part in the filming of Conrad's 'Outcast of the Islands'. From 1946 she traded regularly between Poole and the Channel Islands as a ketch with an auxiliary engine.

144 The *Mountaineer* entering Leghorn in 1858. The *Mountaineer* was Poole's own *Marie Celeste*. She was an 87-ton sloop built at Hamworthy by William Cox and Thomas Slade, Senr. in 1836. In 1850 she was found intact with a cargo of salt 150 miles off Labrador with no one on board or any personal possessions except three miniatures of Princess Alice, Queen Victoria's daughter, in the captain's locker. Channel Island fishermen towed her back to Jersey and, in June 1851, she was registered in the name of Robert Slade, trading as John Slade & Co. In 1858 Henry Taylor whose father was a butcher at the corner shop at Ashley Cross, Parkstone, was boatswain and George Blandford, master, on their journey to Italy.

145 The *Waterwitch*. Built by Thomas Meadus at Hamworthy in 1871, the *Waterwitch* was the last square-rigged merchant ship to carry cargoes from a home port when she was finally discharged at Parr in 1936. She was bought by an Estonian for £400 and was still afloat in the Baltic at the end of the Second World War. A model of her is on display at the National Maritime Museum at Greenwich.

Some Famous Poole Ships

146 *The Lady of Avenel*, a brigantine built at Falmouth in 1874. Reputed to have taken part in the Newfoundland cod trade and the slave trade with Cuba and Brazil before the trade was made illegal in those countries in the late 1880's. Later the ship became a training ship for boys at Falmouth but, in 1925, she was chosen by the British Arctic Expedition and she reached a point nearer to the North Pole than any ship before. She was then brought to Poole where she was converted into a luxury yacht.

147 The *Lady of Avenel* at Holes Bay. She was moved at the beginning of the last war to Holes Bay, the graveyard of so many of Poole's old ships and here the teredo worm gradually destroyed here. Lt/Cdr. Metcalfe, chandler of High Street, bought her oak figurehead and placed it outside his shop where for many years it provided a splash of bright colour to the bottom of High Street. Mr Columbos, who bought the business, later sold the figurehead to a Dutch collector.

148 The *Mary Rose* was commissioned as a training ship for girls by Commander Claude Wollard RN FRGS in 1947 and operated out of Poole very successfully until 1955.

149 The *Etoile*. Many sailing ships, often naval training ships, still come into Poole. This is the French cadet ship *Etoile* on her visit to Poole in 1953. She was visiting Poole with her sister ship, the appropriately-sounding *La Belle Poule*.

150 The Wooden Schooner, 1920. At that time ships were still secured at the Quay by large mooring rings but these were later replaced by bollards. The Wessex Shipyard, shown in the background on the other side of the Quay, built many ships around this period but that year the yard suffered a disastrous loss in its schooner *Pride of the West* being lost on its maiden voyage.

Poole's Lifeboats

151 *The Harmer,* 1912. Poole's lifeboat station at Sandbanks was the first to be established in Dorset. Its first lifeboat was the *Manley Wood* shown in photo 102 of our *Album of Old Poole*. The crew assembled at the Antelope in High Street and were taken by horse-drawn coach to Sandbanks to launch the boat. The original lifeboat was replaced by *Boy's Own No. 2* in 1882 which, in turn, was replaced by *City Masonic* in 1898 and which lasted until *Harmer* took up its duties in Poole in 1913. The *Harmer* served the Poole station until the beginning of the last war.

152 *The Thomas Kirk Wright,* 1939. The *Thomas Kirk Wright* was a slow, shallow boat but was Poole's first motor lifeboat. The lifeboat crew were desperately disappointed with the boat and its slow speed and some of them resigned. However, it did heroic work in bringing out the last troops to be evacuated from Dunkirk when boats of deeper draught could no longer reach the waiting troops. It is now on display in the old lifeboat station off the Fishermen's dock.

153 *The Basset Green,* 1964. The *Basset Green* came from Padstow where it had previously been stationed, in 1964. The lifeboat station, first opened in the Fishermen's dock in July 1882 was recently abandoned for operational use and a position nearer the harbour mouth has been obtained at the Poole Harbour Yatch Club Marina when the *Augustus Courtauld* took over from *Basset Green*.

Poole's Paddlesteamers

154 *The Emperor of India.* Towards the end of the nineteenth century paddle steamers plied regularly in summer between Poole, Swanage, Weymouth, Bournemouth and the Isle of Wight and Southampton. They were operated by Companies in Southampton and Weymouth but Poole harbour was always their berthing place when they were operating locally.

155 *The Monarch.* The Monarch was built in 1888 and owned by Cozens & Co of Weymouth. The steamer operated a service to Cherbourg in 1899 for 7/- return. After the First World War the *Monarch* lost her Cross-Channel Certificate and the run to Cherbourg was taken over by another paddle steamer, the *Balmoral*. The *Monarch* was used for inshore journeys until 1950 when she no longer paid for her keep and was sent to the breakers.

156 The *Embassy* was built in 1911 as the *Duchess of Norfolk*. She was regularly used on the Weymouth – Swanage – Poole – Bournemouth – Isle of Wight run during the summer.

157 The *Bournemouth Queen*, built in Troon in 1908 was a steel ship of 353 tons and put on the Bournemouth – Swanage service. She was towed to Belgium for breaking up at the end of 1957.

Brownsea Island

158, 159 Brownsea Castle c1900. The castle had had to be rebuilt after its disastrous fire of 1896. *The Villano,* the house originally built by Col Waugh for the vicar of St Mary's, is seen in the background past St Andrew's Bay which had been reclaimed for pasture.

The Corporation's consultant on the navigation of the harbour blamed this reclamation for diverting the scour of the tides and causing Little Channel to silt up and said it 'should never have been permitted'.

160 The Italian Winter Garden, Brownsea Castle, 1960. Mrs Bonham-Christie lived her solitary life on Brownsea Island from 1927 until her death in April, 1961. Everything on the island had grown wild, even the once splendid Italian Garden.

163 St Christopher's Plaque, The Quay, Brownsea. George Cavendish-Bentinck owned Brownsea 1871-1891 and had converted the island into a model farm and brought many art treasures to the island. This plaque looks out from Brownsea Quay on all shipping passing into and out of the harbour.

161, 162 Two of the figures in the Italian garden which in 1960 had survived the tangled vegetation which had engulfed them during Mrs Christie's 34 years ownership of the island.

164 St Mary's Church, Brownsea Island, 1903. Built by Col. Waugh in 1854. In the foreground can be seen one of the tees of the 9-hole golf course laid out by Charles Van Raalte around 1902, the year he was Mayor of Poole, for his guests at the castle and for himself and his wife, both of whom played. They even employed a professional, Charlie Major.

165 *God's Acre,* St Mary's Church. Mr Bentinck was buried in God's Acre, as St Mary's churchyard was called, in 1891. His wife Penelope was buried there six years later. The well-head which marks their graves is marked with the crest of the Italian Leza family and is dated 1497.

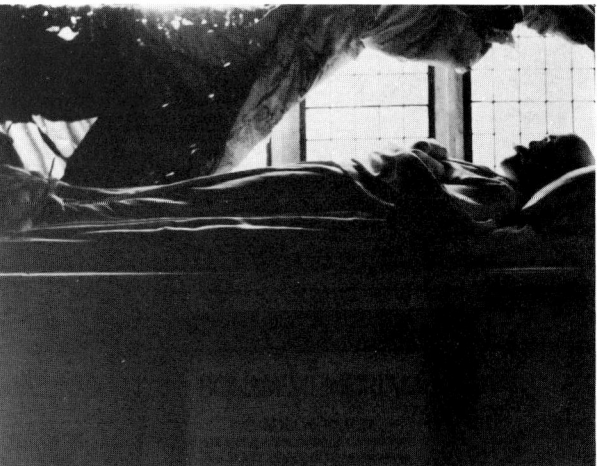

166 Charles Van Raalte's effigy, St Mary's Church. Charles Van Raalte owned Brownsea from 1901 till his death in 1908. He was the second and last man to be elected Mayor of Poole who was not already a member of the Council. Then, as Admiral of the Port, he flew a large burgee from the topmost part of the castle which was duly dipped in salute at the entry or departure of any naval vessel.

167 Royal Mail leaving London.

Communications

Up to the coming of the railway to Hamworthy in 1847 Poole's communications within its own boundaries and with the outside world had hardly changed over the centuries. Within the little town itself there was little need for transport. Any part could easily be reached on foot and, up to 1850 when it was made illegal, the carriage of small quantities of goods was often made through the town's little streets by dog cart drawn by the Newfoundland or Labrador dogs which were first imported into England through Poole.

Longer journeys inland had always depended on the horse. Many of the better-off people of Poole had their own horses and carriages housed in the stables behind their houses. Others could hire a horse or horses with or without a carriage, usually from one of the inns of the town such as The Bulls Head in High Street which had its stables behind the inn facing Lagland Street.

But from the late 18th century regular journeys were made by stage coaches. The Royal Mail coach arrived and left Poole each day and took four passengers. 'The Age' coach set out each morning from the Old Antelope for London via Wimborne, Ringwood and Southampton. Three times a week 'The Wellington' set out for Bristol via Wimborne, Blandford, Shaftesbury, Gillingham, Stourhead and Frome and 'The Independent' called at Poole each day on its regular journey between Weymouth and Southampton. There was, too, a coach which ran three times a week from 'The Angel' to Salisbury.

Poole was also very well served for the transport of goods. In the early 1800's there were 21 established carriers in Poole who made 33 regular runs each week starting from one or other of the many inns and public houses of the town to all the towns of Dorset and Hampshire as well as to London and Bristol.

But the main form of transport of goods at the beginning of the 19th century was still by sea. There were no less than 64 sailing ships regularly carrying freight into and out of Poole in 1846. Some of these, like the hoys which frequently sailed between Poole and Portsmouth (and still remembered from their berth near the Portsmouth Hoy on the Quay) took passengers as well as goods. The stage coaches and the roads improved by the Turnpike Trusts had done little to detract from this sea traffic. But it was very different when the railway came to Poole. By 1852 the 64 ships plying on Poole's coastal trade had shrunk to four. The railway, too, had soon ruined most of the local carriers of goods as well as the coastal shipowners.

The railways even became the main passenger carriers between the local communities when the railway line was extended from Poole to Parkstone, Branksome and Bournemouth West in 1874. By 1885 the traffic had necessitated the laying of a second track.

However, by this time tramways were being laid down in many towns in England. They could operate more frequently and serve localities better than a railway could ever hope to do and, early in the 1890's a private company was formed to lay a horse-drawn tramway between Poole railway station and Bournemouth. However, the Bournemouth Council refused its permission to lay lines through its streets and the company pursued its proposals no further.

In 1899, however, the British Electric Traction Company applied for an order under the Light Railway Act for powers to lay a tramway between Poole station and County Gates to which neither the Branksome or Poole Councils made any objection and the Board of Trade gave its approval. Only the traders of Lower Parkstone objected. Like the Bournemouth Council they objected to the laying of tramlines and overhead wires through 'the village'. The Poole and District Traction Company, a subsidiary formed by the parent company, altered the line of their proposed route to bypass Lower Parkstone and its objectors. At Brown Bottom at the foot of North Road they turned their route up North Road to Constitution Hill and then down Ashley Road into Poole Road to County Gates.

During 1900 the new tramlines and overhead wires were installed at a cost of £64,000 and the company built its depot on the south side of Ashley road, roughly half way on its route. It provided itself with 15 trams, each having a capacity of 48 passengers, 22 on longitudinal seats inside and 26 on the open top. By April, 1901, the lines had been laid to the satisfaction of the Poole Corporation and the Board of Trade's Inspector and its certificate issued.

The new service was opened on 11 April, 1901, an Easter Saturday, and it was inaugurated without the slightest ceremony. No one was present officially from the Poole Corporation and the local newspaper merely mentioned the event on Page 6 of its next edition. There, in the sixth column, between an obituary and an account of a meeting of the Bournemouth Athletic Sports Club, it announced blandly that the service had commenced and that the trams had been crowded over the Easter week-end.

But, despite the official indifferences, the service was an immediate success. The trams, in their livery of Cambridge blue and white, obviously met a public need. The nine-minute service between Poole station and North Road and a similar service between Sea View and County Gates was well patronised – as was the half-hourly connecting service between 'Brown Bottom' and Constitution Hill. This connecting service, in fact, was the only frustration. With the change of route the Company had been able to provide itself with only one tramcar with sufficiently strong brakes safely to be used on the steep slopes of the hill to Sea View and passengers wishing to make the journey from Poole station to County Gates had to change cars twice.

But for all that, the service was so successful that residents and shopkeepers in other areas of Poole were anxious to be served by the new service. The traders of the Old Town petitioned that the tramway should be laid down High Street and, more surprisingly 'The Branksome Park, Sandbanks and Parkstone Extension Association' was formed to urge the extension of the tramway into their areas.

The Poole Company, flushed with success, obtained powers under the Bournemouth and Christchurch Tramways Act to extend the Poole service through Bournemouth to Christchurch. The Company, however, still needed local authority approval to lay tramlines in the streets and the 'Horse Committee' of the Bournemouth Council, then responsible for public transport in the town, refused this permission. It considered that tram lines with their overhead cables and the noise of the trams were quite out of place in Bournemouth.

Despite this decision, the Bournemouth Corporation then promoted its own Act to take powers to operate a tramway service. It was now the turn of the Poole Company to object. It was clear, it argued, that Bournemouth had no intention of establishing a tramway system; they were merely trying to obtain powers to do so in order to strengthen their position to object to anyone else doing so. Parliament was clearly impressed by this argument for, in granting the Bournemouth Council power to operate a tramway service it limited the powers for a period of two years. The powers would expire unless the Corporation had taken substantial action to provide the service by that time.

The following year the Company brought an High Court action alleging that the Bournemouth Council had made so little progress in providing the tram service that it was inconceivable that substantial progress could have been made by the date of the expiry of the powers given by the Act. The Company applied for the Court's declaration that the conditions of the Act had not been complied with and that it was therefore null and void.

Bournemouth Corporation strongly resisted the action, denying that little or no action had been taken to implement its powers, and the High Court accepted their arguments and dismissed the Poole Company's case. The Company was still not satisfied. It appealed to the Court of Appeal which, after a most acrimonious hearing, decided in favour of the Company.

Bournemouth Council now rallied other municipalities to its aid for it was then a matter of civic pride that Borough Councils should run the tram services as a municipal undertaking. They appealed to the House of Lords.

By this time Bournemouth was really pressing on with arrangements to provide a tram service for its town. It was now clear that the Bournemouth Council was dead-set on providing a tramway. The Poole company was in a dilema for it had always argued that it was only logical that local public tramways should be under one control. It therefore suggested to the Bournemouth Council that if it was so adamant that it should run the services in Bournemouth it was only logical that it should buy out the Poole service. Bournemouth agreed in principle.

It was now time for the Poole Corporation to take objection! It could stomach a private company running public transport facilities in Poole, but it could not possibly agree to the Bournemouth Corporation owning a tram depot and tramlines and cables through the main streets of Poole.

After a series of meetings between the three parties it was eventually agreed that it would be the Poole Corporation which would buy out the Poole Company. The Poole Corporation would then let its undertaking to the Bournemouth Corporation who would then become the operator of the Poole undertaking to be run in conjunction with its new Bournemouth system.

The amount which the Poole Corporation should pay for the Poole undertaking was left in abeyance. The Company claimed it was worth £400,000. Poole Corporation considered this price to be grossly exaggerated and, when no agreement could be reached, the matter was referred to arbitration. Finally a figure of £112,000 was fixed, the purchase was completed and the undertaking was leased to the Bournemouth Corporation to operate. The Poole & District Electric Traction Company had lasted only four years and had little to show for its successful pioneering efforts and Poole's 'Bluebells' as the blue and white trams were affectionately known, soon reappeared in their new Bournemouth livery.

The new joint tramway service, with tram lines extended from County Gates through Westbourne into the Square at Bournemouth was opened on 3 July, 1905. Its inauguration was a very different affair from the commencement of the Poole Company's service a few years earlier.

Four single-decker cars, preceded by a 'State Car', all 'tastefully draped' with green, blue, red and white muslin, set off from the new Bournemouth depot on a triumphal journey to the terminus at Poole. At County Gates, then still part of the Branksome Urban District Council, members of that Council were welcomed aboard the cars before they continued on their journey into Poole. At Poole Park the gaily dressed cars stopped and the civic parties alighted to be met by Mr Venables, the Town Sergeant, and conducted to the marquee in the park where they were welcomed by Alderman H F W Gwatkin, the Mayor of Poole. After the official speeches, Mr G W Green, the Poole caterer, provided tea for the 200 civic guests while the D (Poole) Company of the 1st Volunteer Battalion of the Dorchester Regiment 'discoursed a nice selection of music'.

The new tram service continued successfully for the next decade or so. Traders of Lower Parkstone had changed their minds and a new line had been laid from Pottery Junction through Bournemouth Road and Commercial Road to join the original line at Park Gates East. By 1927, however, the local newspaper was complaining that the slow trams were a very second-best to the railways. By this time, too, they were being compared with the motor car. The clanking trams were loud in comparison, and the noise of the tram going up to Constitution Hill at night seemed to reverberate all over the town. Moreover, the increasing number of private motorists were often frustrated by the slow-moving trams which occupied the middle of the road and were frequently stopping for their passengers to alight or board.

By 1928 the tramlines laid through Lower Parkstone needed relaying and the Bournemouth Corporation told the Poole Corporation that the service could not continue unless new lines were provided. But Poole had become disenchanted with its trams. The Corporation decided that the expense of relaying the lines was not worthwhile and the service through Lower Parkstone came to an end in January, 1929 after only 21 years' operation. The Poole Corporation negotiated an agreement with the Hants and Dorset Omnibus Company to operate a bus service over this route.

In 1934 the Bournemouth Tramways and Motor Service (as it had been renamed) started replacing its trams by trolley buses. It decided that trolley buses should also replace the trams on the Poole services. But it was now the turn of the Poole Corporation to decide it was not in the interests of Poole that its streets should any longer be festooned with wires. Moreover, by this time, it had had a few years' experience of the operation of motor buses and considered them superior to trolley buses. It refused its sanction to the substitution of its trams by trolley buses.

It was probably a lucky coincidence that the original lease of the Poole tramway undertaking had been for thirty years from 1905. This allowed the Poole Corporation to negotiate terms with the Hants and Dorset Company to take over and extend the Poole services.

The terms agreed with the Hants and Dorset Company were that the Company would pay the Corporation £75,000 for the assets and for the right to operate buses over the 'prescribed routes' of the original order and that the Company would pay to the Corporation each year a sum equal to 10% of the profits arising on these routes. The Hants and Dorset Company has provided public transport services in Poole ever since that time.

168 Mr J S Flower of Branksome Hotel Stables, 1914 offered to provide 'well-horsed landaus, broughams, victorias, brakes, single and pair horse omnibuses of all kinds for evening parties as well as light vans for luggage.

The Trains

169 A Goods train with 0-4-0 tank engine at Hamworthy Goods station shortly before it was finally closed in 1956.

170 Mr Langdown, 1896. When the Hamworthy Station was closed to passenger traffic in 1896 Mr Langdown remained there as first porter at the then exclusively goods station.

171 Poole Railway Station from Towngate Street, 1959. When the railway first came to Poole it was only a single line until 1885 and, until 1893, passengers for London still had to go via Wimborne.

172 The new Towngate road bridge necessitated the demolition of the station. A new station was built a little lower down the line.

The Trams

173 The inaugural photograph of the staff of the Poole & District Electric Traction Co. with their tramcars at the Company's new depot in Ashley Road, Upper Parkstone.

174 A 'Bluebell' en route for the Poole terminus. The lines were laid in the middle of the road with extra loop-lines so that tramcars could pass each other. Otherwise the trams went both ways on the same line.

175 A 'Bluebell' in Parkstone Road, 1902, taken from near Poole Park's *Middle Gates* which had to be shut some 60 years later to avoid traffic congestion there.

The Trams

176 The Longfleet interchange, 1902. No. 17 tram had to wait while the outgoing tram passed it on the loop line.

177 The Tram shelter, Brown Bottom, 1903. The Company provided substantial shelters for its passengers. This was their shelter provided at the foot of North Road on the spot where the island is now situated outside the Municipal Offices. The clock to the left is a 'Bundy Clock' which the conductors of each tram had to punch on arrival so that their times could be checked.

178 The Tram Shelter remained for many years at what became known as Park Gates East. It then was placed on land between Wimborne and Garland Roads and then moved to Baiter on land at the back of the Fishermens' Dock as a shelter where it was gradually destroyed by vandalism.

179 Alderman and Mrs J E Beale, Mayor and Mayoress of Bournemouth, being escorted to the marquee to meet the Mayor of Poole at the opening of the Bournemouth Corporation Tramway service, 3 July, 1905.

180 The tea party in Poole Park, given by Ald Gwatkin, Mayor of Poole, to celebrate the opening of the tramway service between the two towns, 1905.

181 When the ceremonial trams had dropped their passengers at the park they went on to wait at the Poole terminus. Mr Wilkins, the photographer, seems to have got most of the drivers and conductors into his picture. The conductors were then paid 27/6d (£1.37½) for a 60-hour week with an annual bonus of 4/- (20p) for good behaviour. The fare from Longfleet to Bournemouth Square was then 5d (2p).

182 The Tram terminus and shelter at Longfleet in 1930. The standards shown at each side of the level crossing supported the electric cable for the tramcars. When the trams ceased to run most of them were used as light standards. They gradually became dangerous as they rusted from inside and were gradually replaced but the last one was not removed until 1971. The High Street level crossing can be seen a little further up the line.

183 A last tram car in Ashley Road, 1935.

184 Map of Poole, 1760.

Some other old Poole Streets

The residents of old Poole had little need for quick transport within the town or, for that matter, into or out of the town. The three main lateral roads of the town, West Street, Market Street and High Street all ended before they reached the northern boundary of the town and facilities for cross traffic between them was poor. The only way out of the town for a long time was by way of the Town Gates and the drawbridge over the deep ditch which had been dug to connect the waters of Parkstone Bay with Longfleet Bay, as Holes Bay was then known. The only moderately reasonable way to cross the town, apart from the Quay itself, was by way of Strand Street and Fish (Castle) Street.

Larger residential development had started round St James and spread out into West Street, High Street and New Street. At the time of the map in 1760 Poole had already achieved its early mansion houses at 87 High Street and 13 Thames Street but about that time was when the merchants of the town were vying with each other to build bigger and more elaborate mansions and it was around this time that 8 New Street, 32 West Street, 127 and 129 High Street, 20 Market Street, West End House and Peter Thompson's house in Pillory Street were built. The smaller property was built on the eastern side of the town, starting with Strand Street.

The early seat of town affairs was centred round Fish Street where the Town Hall and prison and the main hostelry, the Rising Sun, were situate. It was the year after the plan was drawn that the Poole Corporation was offered the money to build a new meat market. The appropriate place for it was obviously in Market Street, then the main shopping and business street of the town. The Burgesses took advantage of this offer to build a new Town Hall for themselves on the top of the new market. In building the Guildhall in Market Street in 1761 the centre of the town affairs was transferred to Market Street. This move took away much of the old importance of Fish Street.

185 Avenue Place. Almost every corner of the old town was the site of a small shop which would sell in very small quantities. The Ridouts had been butchers in Poole for many generations.

West Street   West Side

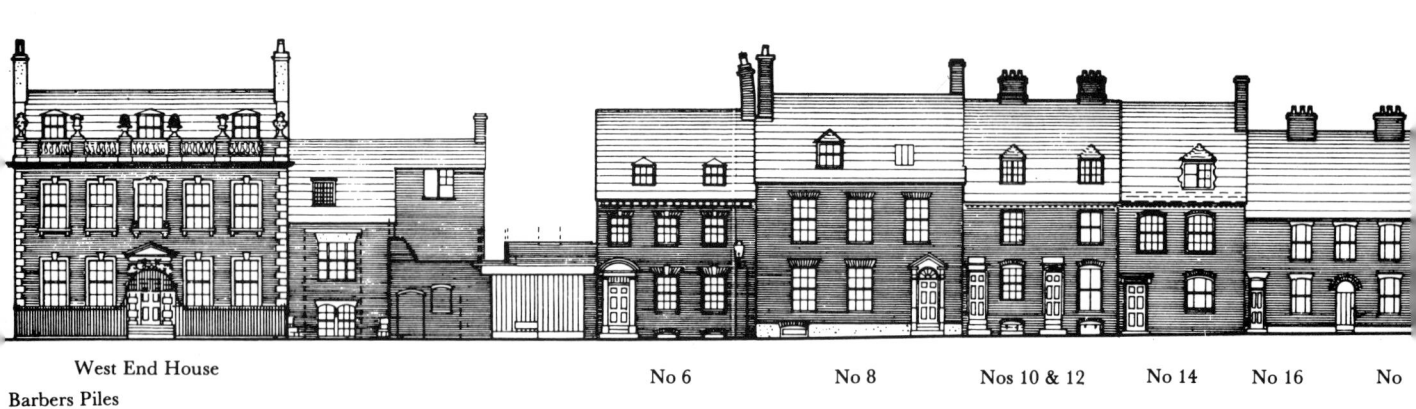

West End House / Barbers Piles — No 6 — No 8 — Nos 10 & 12 — No 14 — No 16 — No

186 A mid-18th century merchant's house, built by the Slades. It was in a garage at the rear of the house that Owen Carter carried out experiments in the design of vases, bowls and dishes which, fired at Poole Pottery, first brought the Pottery into artistic prominence about the turn of the century.

187 Nos. 22 – 28 West Street. The two white-faced houses were built about 1700. No. 24 was built by David Durell, a Poole ship's captain and merchant. Later other well-known Poole merchants, Thomas Hyde, Benjamin Linthorpe and Stephen Adey, lived there. In 1922 Giovanni Zollo bought it for £500 to convert it into a lodging house. He died in 1932 but his widow and son Angelo continued the business until 1957. They took up to 30 lodgers at 24s/6d a week.

West Street   West Side

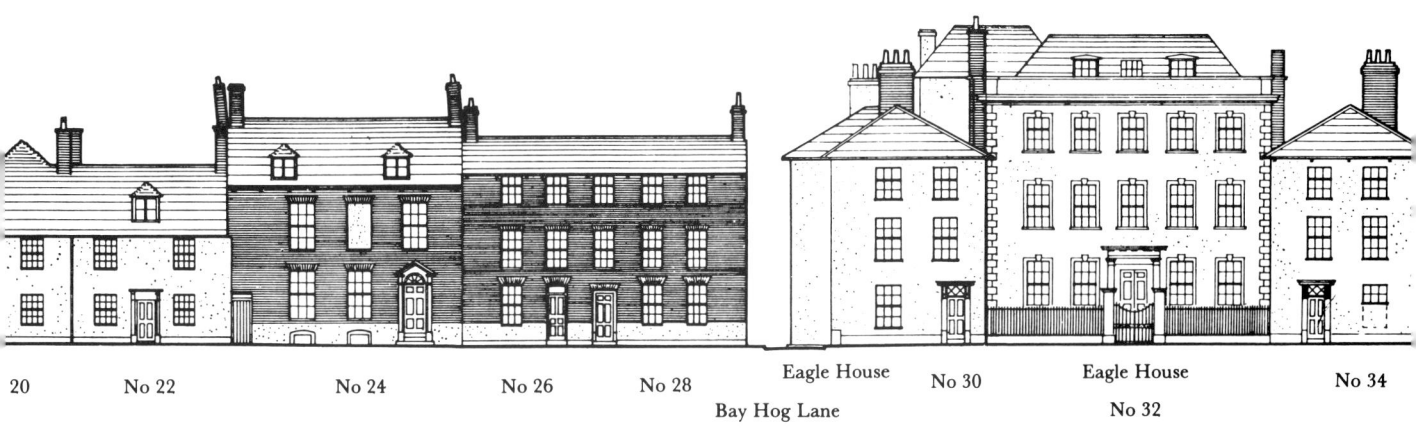

20   No 22   No 24   No 26   No 28   Eagle House   No 30   Eagle House   No 34
                                             Bay Hog Lane   No 32

188 Georgian ironwork, West Street. Most of the Georgian mansions built by the Newfoundland merchants had ironwork of this kind, a feature of it being the cast iron knobs.

190 Dorset House in about 1900. From the 1890's the house was used as a home for orphan girls. It was bought by Brownsea Haven Properties in 1934 and sold to Usher's Brewery in 1963 who converted its large rear garden to a lorry loading area for its premises next door which they had built after one of the Slades' houses had been demolished in the last war – by a bomb which had done little damage to Dorset House apart from destroying the old Jolliffe eagles on the gateway.

189 Jolliffe House was used as a wine store by the Haven Hotel for many years and was known as The Haven Cellars until 1963.

191 Eagle House, 1873. In 1750 William Jolliffe left his 'newly erected dwellinghouse in West Street' to his eldest son Peter. Peter reclaimed a large area of mudland off his back garden and built a wharf and coal yard there. Peter's heir, Rev Peter William Jolliffe, sold the house. Later, in 1815, it was bought by Christopher Jolliffe. By this time a highway West Quay Road, had been established on the 'West Shore'. In 1831 Christopher Jolliffe went bankrupt and G R Robinson MP bought the house and added the north and south wings. In 1966 it became the property of a member of the Jolliffe family for the third time when Mrs R Allenby bought it and renamed it Jolliffe House.

West Street   East Side

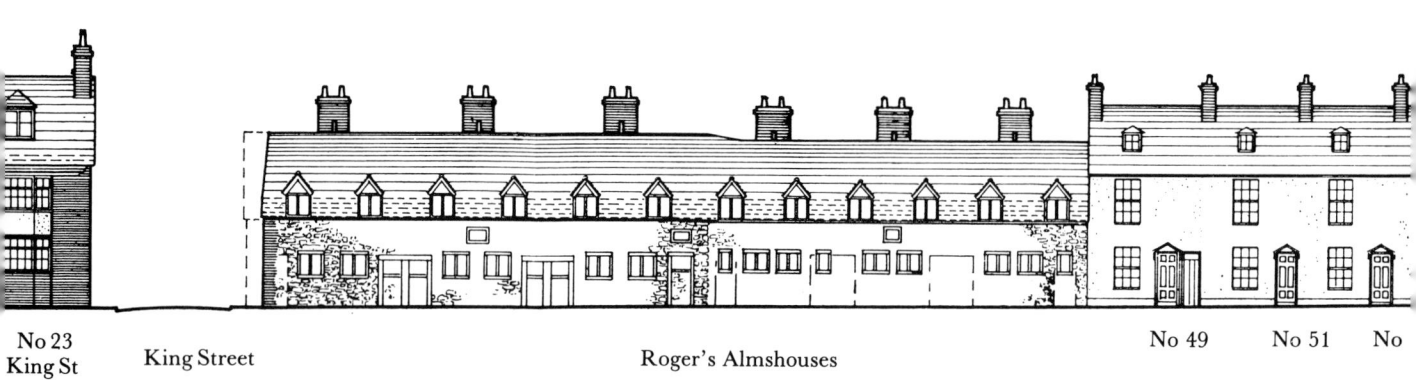

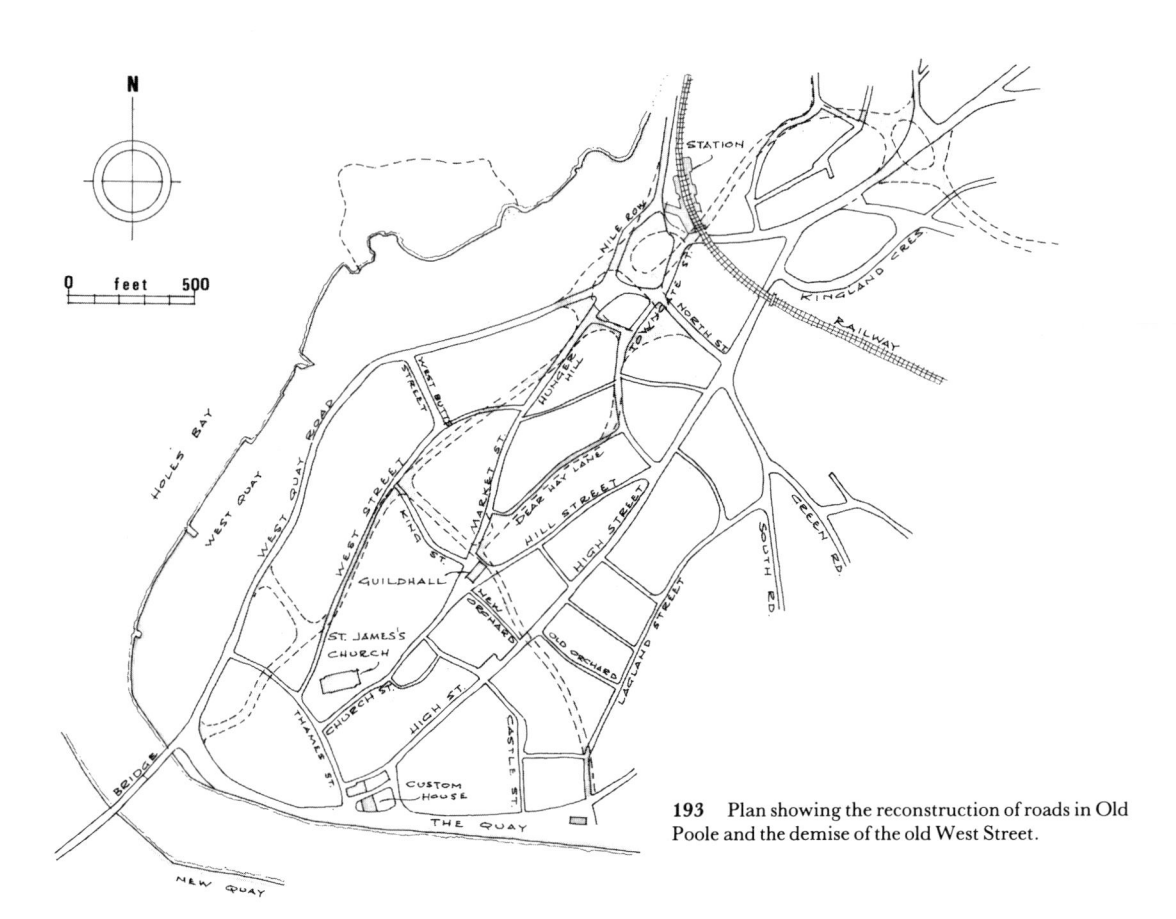

| No 23 King St | King Street | Roger's Almshouses | No 49 | No 51 | No |

193 Plan showing the reconstruction of roads in Old Poole and the demise of the old West Street.

192 Roger's Almshouses. Robert Rogers was a native of Poole who became a prosperous leather merchant near London and left many charitable gifts at his death. One of these was one of 500 marks (£333) to then Poole Corporation to build almshouses for six poor couples of Poole. The Corporation built six almshouses on land in West Street at a cost of £158. 16. 4d. They then bought land at Merley for £292 (adding the balance from their own funds) to produce a rent sufficient to give each couple 12d a week, paid each Sunday 'in the great porch of the church at Poole'.

A tablet was built into the Almshouses which read: *1604. Fundatore Roberto Rogers apud Londinensis pellione Polae nato*.

In the early 1800's the six almshouses were divided into twelve tenements, the inmates receiving 6d each week plus coal at Christmas.

Skinner Street

194 'The Independent Chapel', Skinner's Field. The Congregational Chapel (now the United Reform Church) on the north side of Skinner Street was built in 1777. A vestry was added in 1814 and the chapel extended in 1823 when the galleries were added which allowed 1500 people to be accommodated. The Infants School was added in 1834. The interior was renovated and reseated in 1880. The burial ground was on the north side.

Lagland Street

195 The Friends' Meeting House. George Fox, the founder of the Society of Friends, visited Poole in 1655 and again in 1657 and 1658. He wrote of Poole that 'there is becoming a great gathering in the name of Jesus, of a very tender people who continue under Christ's teaching'. Many of Poole's leading citizens became Quakers. The building is now used as a Boys' Club.

196 Lagland Street in 1910. This area of Poole probably had a greater density of residents than any other area.

197 Lagland Street in 1957. Little had changed in the 17 years since the previous photograph had been taken.

Castle Street   South-West Side

No 10   Strand Street   No 12   No 14   No 16   No 18   No 20   No 22   No 24   No 26   No 28

198 Castle Street runs up from the Quay and turns to enter High Street opposite the old Corn Market. It was at the bottom of this street that the Poole men fought the Spanish and French invaders in 1405 when they attacked Poole to avenge the exploits of Poole's privateer, Harry Paye, against their shipping. The street then became known as Pluddie or Bloody Street, a name later changed to Fish Street. Then, in the 1930's, the name was changed to Castle Street for no apparent reason.

199 The Rising Sun was built about 1600 as a large hostelry comprising Nos. 14, 16, 18 and 20 Castle Street as well as the little Public House shown as the Rising Sun in this photograph of 1958. The Inn's business fell off when the Guildhall was built in Market Street and gradually most of the premises of the old inn were converted into separate dwellings units and the remaining business was concentrated in the old alehouse of the inn.

Castle Street   South-West Side

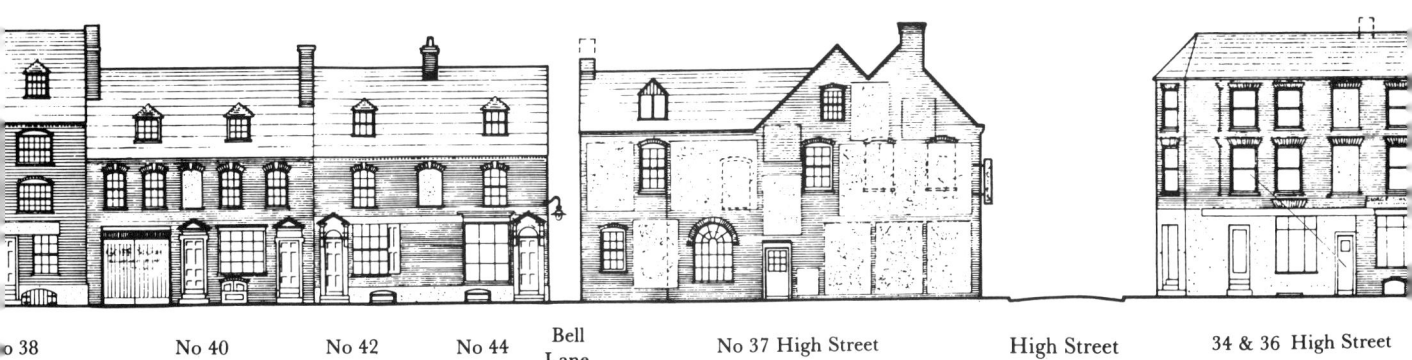

No 38   No 40   No 42   No 44   Bell Lane   No 37 High Street   High Street   34 & 36 High Street

200 A little further down Castle Street. High Street is at the end of the property shown in this photograph. Few of the houses were now used as such. Some had been converted into warehouses and most were in a quite ruinous condition by 1959.

Castle Street

High Street
(Corn Market)

No 39

201 The Salvation Army Citadel, 1960. The Salvation Army came to Poole in 1879. It first used the Temperence Hall in Hill Street for its Sunday services and the Friends Meeting Room for its week-day meetings. It often had 1000 people at its Sunday services. Opponents raised a 'Skeleton Army' whose only objective was to oppose the work of the Army and to disrupt their meetings. They even managed to knock off General Booth's top hat once as he led a procession through Poole. On another occasion the Riot Act was read and the leader of the Skeleton Army was imprisonned. The Army claimed to have converted him on their visits to him in prison.

The Salvation Army remained in this building until 1972 when its present building was erected near to its original home at the Temperence Hall.

North-East Side

No 29   No 27

202 Harman's Yard, 1958. The old Town Hall was built in the middle of Fish Street in 1572. It was demolished in 1761 and its site added to the road. After the war the old building shown in the photograph was used by H Harmon & Co, 'iron, scrap and metal merchants'. It had on its wall a tablet unveiled by Cr. W J Stickland, Mayor of Poole, to mark the bi-centenary of the evangelical conversion of John Wesley, Founder of Methodism, who had been imprisoned in the old prison under the old Town Hall, for offending against Charles II's 'Five Mile Act'.

203 The Old Bell Inn, 1958. The old inn had been divided in the late 1700's into two and the south part raised to two stories.

South Street

204 Lewen's Iron and Brass Foundry. Situtated on the corner of Lagland Street and Green Road, the foundry was probably then the most extensive building of the town. In 1876, however, fire destroyed much of it. It finally closed in 1900.

205 Butler's Brush Factory, 1960. Brush making was for long a flourishing trade of Poole. It first started in premises next to the Antelope Hotel in High Street and later by Mr Hayman near Miles & Sons' shop in High Street. Butlers took over the remaining premises of Lewen's foundry in 1906 as a brush factory. However, in 1955 it suffered another disastrous fire and was never rebuilt. The premises were bought by the Corporation and the site used partly for road improvement and partly as an extension to the grounds of South Road school.

206 Poole's First Free Library. This part of South Road was previously known as Great Mount Street, a name later contrac to Mount Street as shown on the name plate, still on the wall of House.

A Guide to Poole, published in the late 1880's, stated 'Not much can be said for the public buildings of the town. The Guildhall in Market Street is an old building of the last centu It serves its purpose, perhaps, of affording accommodation t municipal, magisterial and trading habits of the town, but a stranger will not linger over its classical architecture, or be enthused by its commanding appearance. A far more attractiv building is the recently erected Free Library and School of Art. This fine property was also the gift to the town, the donor bein John J Norton Esq . . . its architectural style is 'Queen Anne'.'

Baiter Street

East Street

207 At the time of this photograph in 1962 Baiter Street was known as Pound Street. It shows coal being transported from the Quay through the lower part of the town to the Gasworks at Pitwines.

208 A view of the eastern end of Old Poole in 1960 from the newly erected flats in East Street. The Gasworks buildings are in the background of the photograph.

Poole Lanes

209 Blue Boar Lane, 1957.

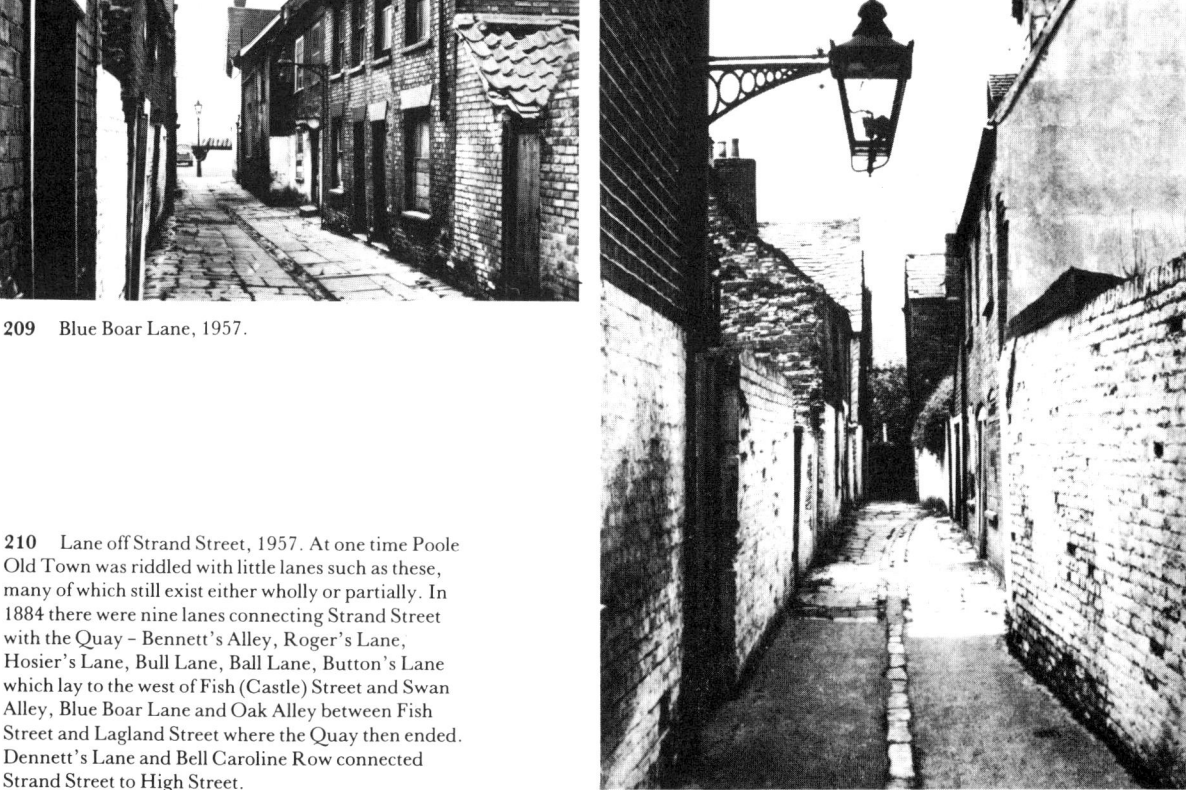

210 Lane off Strand Street, 1957. At one time Poole Old Town was riddled with little lanes such as these, many of which still exist either wholly or partially. In 1884 there were nine lanes connecting Strand Street with the Quay – Bennett's Alley, Roger's Lane, Hosier's Lane, Bull Lane, Ball Lane, Button's Lane which lay to the west of Fish (Castle) Street and Swan Alley, Blue Boar Lane and Oak Alley between Fish Street and Lagland Street where the Quay then ended. Dennett's Lane and Bell Caroline Row connected Strand Street to High Street.

West Quay Road

211 Garland's Almshouses. This range of almshouses at the corner of Hunger Hill and West Quay Road was built by George Garland, Poole merchant, in 1814 and given to the Corporation with an endowment of £200, the interest on which was to be spent on repairs with any balance to be paid over annually to the tenants on Christmas eve. In 1822 George Garland added two rented houses in Market Street to the endowment with the stipulation that two-thirds of the rentals were to be divided between the tenants on the first Monday of each month and the balance retained for repairs. The site of the almshouses is now lost in the Hunger Hill roundabout and the site of Towngate Bridge.

212 The Church of St Mary and St Philomena. The Catholics of Poole built the Chancel and Nave of this church on the West Shore in 1839. The building was considerably enlarged about the turn of this century by the addition of the isles on each side and a vestry and porch. It was originally approached by way of 'Catholic Lane', later New Street. The site was acquired by the Corporation when the new Catholic Church was built. The Corporation sold the site to the RNLI for the erection of its new Headquarters.

Hill Street

213 Looking down Hill Street towards the Guildhall from Carters Lane in 1962. The Temperence Hall is on the left just past the white faced house. In No. 31 Hill Street William Parker Snow was born in 1817. He became famous as an author and an early Arctic explorer.

214 New Orchard. The original New Orchard was a narrow road running from High Street to Market Street just below the Guildhall. The new New Orchard was built to connect Lagland Street, High Street and West Quay Road north of the Guildhall.

Some Old Poole characters

215 The 'Grand Old Man of Poole' c. 1890. George Curtis, estate agent and builder, worked as a temperance advocate and sabbatarian all his life after qualifying as a Wesylan preacher when he was only 21. He was Mayor of Poole in 1880 and again in 1906 and 1907. He habitually wore a top hat and frock coat long after they had gone out of fashion. Although his firm did considerable building, including the Water Tower in Upper Parkstone, he was best known as an estate agent and lay preacher.

216 The 'Dockers' Seat' in High Street, 1950. Prior to the last war there were 200 dockers employed in the port. Their numbers greatly decreased during the war and afterwards.

217 Italian Organ Grinder, 1952. 'Papa' Benedetto came back from his service in H.M. Forces in the First World War to his peregrinating organ grinding but by 1952 his monkey had had to be put down and his trade was hardly supporting him. Children remained at school for their midday meal, wives were often away from home at work and the radio dispensed a new kind of music. There were few left who were willing to encourage 'Papa' to continue.

218 Knife Grinder, 1953. At one time before the war there were so many travelling salesmen hawking their wares round the houses of the town that it became usual for occupiers to fix metal plates on their gates bluntly stating 'No hawkers, no peddlars, no circulars' John Saunders, pictured here, struggled on after the war for a long time despite the advent of saw-edged knives and electric knife sharpeners.

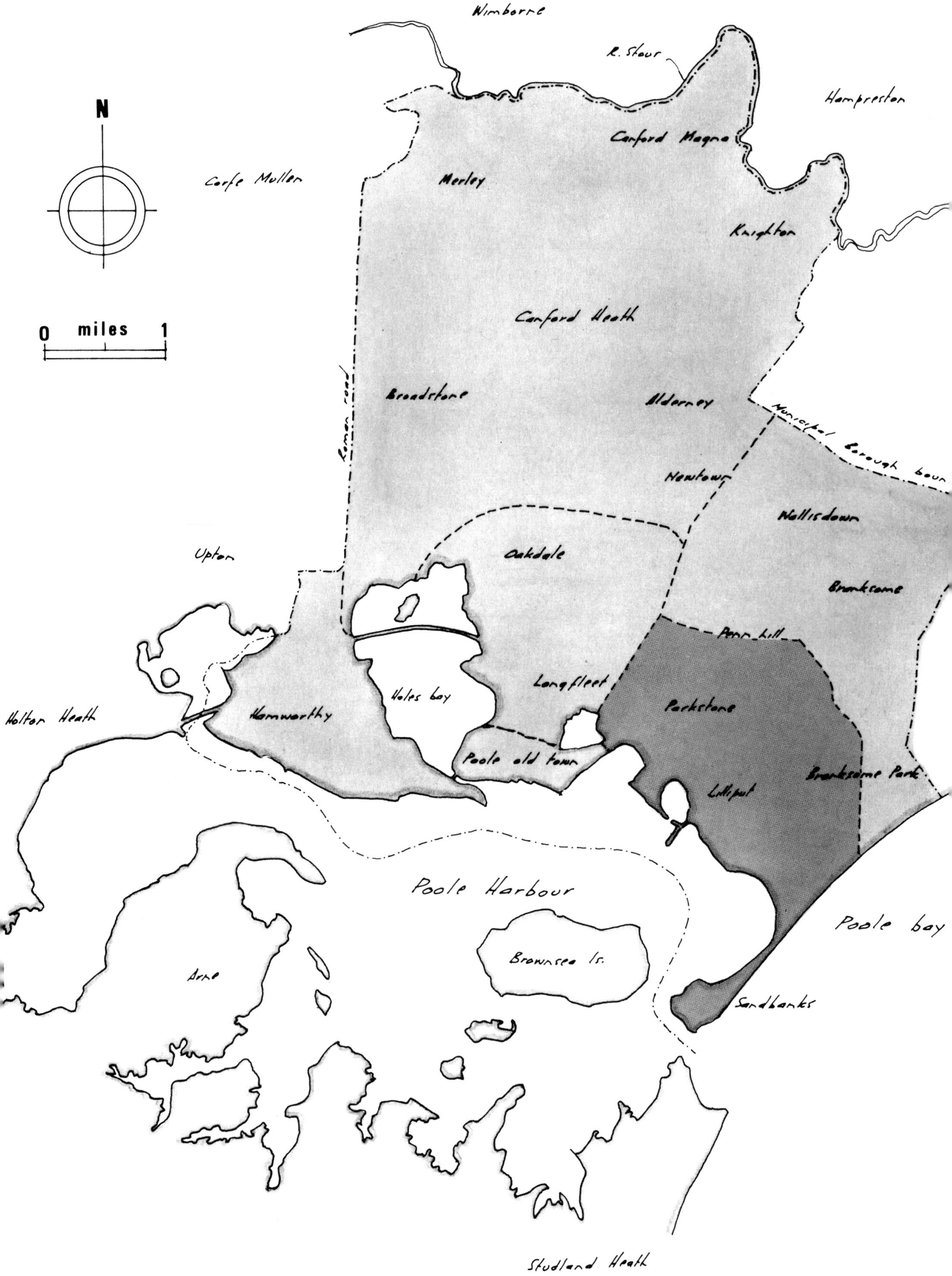
Wimborne
R. Stour
Hampreston
N
Corfe Mullen
Canford Magna
Merley
Knighton
0 miles 1
Canford Heath
Roman road
Broadstone
Alderney
Municipal Borough boun
Newtown
Wallisdown
Upton
Oakdale
Branksome
Penn hill
Longfleet
Holes bay
Holton Heath
Hamworthy
Parkstone
Poole old town
Branksome Park
Lilliput
Poole Harbour
Poole bay
Brownsea Is.
Arne
Sandbanks
Studland Heath

Parkstone

In the Universal British Directory of 1798 the area surrounding Poole was described as "a barren, dreary heath which affords no pleasant view to travellers who come from the more delightful parts of the country."

This most surprising condemnation of Parkstone and the surrounding areas was to some extent borne out by an old coachman writing of his memories of Parkstone in the year that Victoria came to the throne. He wrote:

"Parkstone in 1837 was a picturesque little hamlet. The new Christchurch Road led through it eastwards from Gost's Bay, as Parkstone Bay was then called.

"There was then a Bee Hive Tavern and a Brittania Inn where frequent cock fights were held and, far away on the cliffs at the sandbanks was Mr Aldrick's house, the captain of the coastguards, – and in a dangerous position it was for a house. In fact the sea undermined the cliff and the house fell to pieces.

"Going towards Christchurch from Ashley Cross the people were very industrious. In Notting's Buildings by the new Post Office, dozens of men, women and children made boots and shoes as well as fishing nets, woollen clothing etc. which Mr Slade and other merchants shipped to Newfoundland.

"As the coaches went up the hill out of Parkstone, on the right was 'Castle Eve' where Capt Byce lived and, over the top was 'Sandecotes', built by Mr Daw. Above 'Castle Eve' Capt Festing lived, then the best-known man in Parkstone, who married the widow of 'The Elms' and built a house with a beautiful view called 'Highmoor', later occupied by Rev Parr, the vicar of Parkstone.

"On the left as you left Parkstone there were only four houses – a thatched cottage and, above it, in a sequestered nook in the trees, a house with a terrace and verandah built by Mr Patzka who married a wealthy Poole widow. He had chosen what most people agreed was the best site in the parish for his house. Behind his house was 'Belmont', owned by 'Merchant Brown' and, further up the hill, you could see 'The Castle', a curious, fancy place like a border fortress 'in small'.

"Then, at the top of what was then known as Parkstone Hill but later became known as Castle Hill after the 'fortress in small', we see little but bare heath and long lines of fir trees with scarcely a house, apart from the turnpike."

By the time he was writing, however, at the time of Victoria's Jubilee, the railway had come to Parkstone and that year it had achieved its second line. Parkstone had also achieved its Post Office and its own postal area when postcards could be posted with a $\frac{1}{2}$d stamp and be delivered locally the same day. The saltings of Parkstone were then a thing of the past but the older Parkstone residents were complaining bitterly that the district round the old saltings was getting to be referred to as 'Lilliput' rather than by its old name of 'The Saltings'. The manufacture of nets and stockings had gone by 1887 as had the old cultivation of mulberry trees and the old local custom of gathering samphire (St Pierre's herb) which had been generally used for pickling.

By 1887, however, some shops had appeared in Parkstone village and 'Three Acre Field' had been acquired by the Corporation for an open space. There had been considerable local discussion on what use should be made of it; how best it could be laid out, and how to deal with the little stream which ran through it. With the Jubilee of Queen Victoria the area for a time became known as The Victoria Ground but eventually it was decided that the land would best be used as a 'somewhat refined village green' and became known as Parkstone Park.

At that time, too, some of the footpaths of the village were being asphalted and the Poole Corporation considered the time had come when the roads of the village should be named. Its first efforts to name the Parkstone roads, however, met with little local approval. It is not difficult to understand the residents' views for the first roads to be named were called 'Constitution Hill Road East', 'Conduit Street' and the road from 'Oak Corner' to the railway station was called 'Church Street South'! None of these names survived the villagers' disapproval.

By the time of Victoria's Jubilee Parkstone had already started to grow as the Castle Eve and Sandecotes Estates were developed. It was a common saying then that 'Wareham was, Poole is, and Parkstone will be.' But inevitably as Parkstone expanded some things were lost to the residents as well as gained. The favourite local walks through the Sandecotes Woods were lost as development extended. Eventually only a small area around Stromboli Hill overlooking the area which was to become the Parkstone Golf Course was left as an open space.

Parkstone had long ago shaken off any possible criticism that it was barren heath. It prided itself that it was the 'Mentone of England'. The local press in 1867 went even further. In an editorial fulminating against the devastation of the trees of Parkstone for export as pit props for South Wales, it argued that it was the trees of Parkstone and Bournemouth which made these areas so much better than Brighton, Dover, Hastings and Eastbourne where 'the effect of glaring colours and the excessive light of the cliffs counterbalanced the advantages of climate'. On the other hand, in Parkstone, the trees 'moderate, without excluding the warmth; in winter protect the district from north winds and the leaves, cones and branches form a light, dry soil particularly favourable to consumptive patients.' In fact the Press went further. 'Nice is exposed to sharp winter winds from the Alps,' it wrote, 'Bournemouth and Parkstone are entirely protected and are therefore better than Nice, Cannes, Mentone, Montpelier and the south coast of France and Italy.'

220 Springdale House gave its name to the nearby roads. Originally it was the home of William Pearce, owner of Poole Foundry and one of the principal land owners of Parkstone as well as the chief proprietor of the old Poole Waterworks Company. He was mayor of Poole in 1847, 1858 and 1868. He died in 1899 but his widow continued to live in the house till her own death. It then became the Dorchester School but was finally closed and demolished in 1964.

221 The 'Castle', Castle Hill. The 'Fortress in small' built on Parkstone Hill and which eventually changed the name of the hill to Castle Hill.

Parkstone

222 Parkstone Park was opened in 1888. The Corporation exchanged lands with Lord Wimborne to achieve the land for the park, both pieces being then valued at £1,200. It cost the Corporation £560 to lay it out as a 'somewhat refined village green'.

223 Ashley Cross, the main crossroads of Parkstone 'village'. Parkstone in 1890 was growing fast and in that year municipal offices were built on the corner of Britannia Road and Salterns Road with a Committee room, a fire station 'with accommodation for a manual engine, horse cart, hose reel and fire escape and drying tower for hose'. There was also stabling for four horses, a house for the steam roller, mess room for the men, store rooms and sundry sheds – all for £1,900! For many years now the building has been used as a branch library.

224 Bonnett's Store, 1912. There were a few shops to the east of Parkstone Park among which was Bonnett's store 'where everything for the table in the form of fish (directly from the boats each morning), poultry and game to the best groceries and provisions are obtainable.' The shop sent out a weekly price list, called daily for orders and promised 'to carry out requirements precisely and to delivery with promtitude.'

225 A little higher up Castle Hill Messrs Turner and Walter had taken over the old Parkstone Hall for their garage business. It had previously been used as a place of entertainment and for public meetings. It was here that Alderman Carter, as Mayor, introduced Winston Churchill to a political meeting when he came to speak in support of his friend and cousin, Capt 'Freddie' Guest, when he was a Liberal candidate for Poole.

Parkstone

226 'Poole Road', Parkstone, 1906. Commercial Road before the tramlines were laid showing the Congregational Chapel with its spire.

227 The congregational Chapel, built in 1893. Rev. Willoughby Gee was minister there 1903 – 1917.

228 Sandbanks Road was originally the main road from Poole to the east. After skirting Parkstone Bay it turned east and later cut north near Elgin Road to reach Penn Hill. By the time of the photograph, however, the main road east had long been the main road through Parkstone village.

Parkstone

229 The harbour from Whitecliff, 1948. The old Powder House on Baiter can just be seen on the right. In the Napoleonic wars the Poole merchantmen armed themselves to repel capture but, to guard against possible explosions at the Quay, on entering port they unloaded their explosives at the Powder House, well away from the Quay.

230 Whitecliff, c1900. Whitecliff was at one time a favourite place for picnics and outings.

231 Parkstone Sailing Club, c1900. It was established on the promontory opposite Whitecliff and approached at the side of the 'Elms' by way of Turks Lane.

232 South Western Pottery, 1912. The Pottery existed for many years to the north of Parkstone Cemetery and off Pottery Road. Coal was once brought to the pottery from Saltern's Pier by a light railway. It crossed Sandbanks Road near the Beehive Hotel. The finished products of the Company were transported by the South Western Railway by way of a loop line laid from Parkstone Station which came to a point near the end of the present South Western Road.

233 Clay Cutters, 1912. The clay was cut by hand to a fixed depth. The depths of the cuts can be seen on the clay face. The spades were lubricated by first throwing water into the cut. The man on the left is using a 'pug', a spiked fork, with which he pitched about a hundred weight of clay into the trolley. It was said that the pug-man would deal with over 100 tons of clay a day in this way.

234 Parkstone Golf course from Stromboli Hill, 1912. In digging the reservoirs for the old private Poole waterworks, the Company spread the spoil alongside the Luscombe stream, a mound which is still a feature of some of the gardens of houses on the east side of Compton Avenue. The reservoirs were abandoned in 1909 and acquired by Lord Wimborne with the old pump house in exchange for the balance of Ladies Walking Field at Longfleet and incorporated in his new golf club. At the same time it was agreed that the Corporation and Lord Wimborne would share the cost of building a new road on the western side of the reservoirs running towards Sandbanks, a road which is now Compton Avenue and Bingham Avenue.

235 Parkstone Golf Club House, 1912. Stromboli Hill is to the left of the lady in the photograph, the Luscombe stream in front of her. The Golf Course, designed by Willie Park, was opened in 1910. Lady Cornelia Wimborne banned play on the course on Sundays.

236 Lilliput Road, 1912. The lady in the previous photograph, presumably the photographer's wife, had had a long walk from her earlier position near the first tee to this point on what was to become Lilliput Road near the 4th tee. The area to her right was then known as Pigeon Bottom and the area at the top of the hill to her right was known as 'Compton Acre'.

Lilliput

237 Looking from Evening Hill over the harbour and Sandbanks in 1957. Old Harry Rocks are in the distance.

238 Lilliput, 1890. A view over the old Parkstone saltings to Salterns Lane, now the Blue Lagoon.

Canford Cliffs

239 Canford Cliffs Road, 1912. The road along the brow of Spur Hill to Canford Cliffs.

240 West Hill, Canford Cliffs, 1912. At the turn of the century roads were laid out to form Canford Cliffs 'village' and the roads were named after the earlier lord of the manor (W F S Ponsonby who became Lord de Mauley) and the trustees of his estate. The Rev. Walter Ponsonby, installed as Rector of Canford, inherited the family title of the Earl of Bessborough. Bessborough and de Mauley Roads were two of the main roads of the estate. St Clair, Beaumont, Bodley and Langdown were named after the trustees of the estate, through Langdown Road was later changed to MacAndrew Road.

  The estate's longest road was originally Flaghead Road which led in a straight line from the centre of the estate to the harbour not far from Flag Head. Its original course was at the side of the Church of the Transfiguration. At this point, however, it proved too steep for horse traffic and West Hill was built, bending the road north of the steepest part of the hill. Later most of Flaghead Road was renamed Haven Road and the old road past the church became disused and was reduced to a footpath.

241 Simpson's Folly, 1881. The 1885 Post Office Directory found only two features of Canford Cliffs to be noteworthy. The first was the medical spring near Flag Head, the water of which was said to contain iron, sulphur and iodine. The second was that 'houses especially suited for retired bathing and yatching boxes will be built with every care for their sanitary efficiency in accordance with the views of Dr R W Richardson FRS as practically illustrated in a concrete house erected on the undercliff. Lord Wimborne, who is lord of the manor, Lord Alington and John Hawkins Simpson, Esq. are the principal landowners.'

By 1890 Mr Simpson was no longer a principal landowner. He had been replaced by Edward H Solly.

242 Simpson's Folly, 1953. The Coastguards had blown up Mr Simpson's house when it became dangerous but the enormous slabs of concrete defied the ravages of the sea as they lay strewn over the foreshore of Canford Cliffs for over 70 years before they were incorporated in the new promenade built in 1963.

243 A drawing of Canford Cliffs from the sea in 1865 to illustrate a water spout which had appeared in the sea. The only other building, apart from the Martello Tower at Canford Cliffs was then probably the manor's hunting lodge built at the side of what became Elmstead Road.

Canford Cliffs

244 Canford Cliffs Hotel and Martello Tower c1900. At first the hotel had unrestricted views over Poole Bay to the entrance to the harbour and flourished until the Second World War when it was burnt out by an incendiary bomb attack. Only its stables remained intact and they were later converted into the Canford Cliffs public house, lately renamed The Nightjar.

245 Canford Cliffs Chine and its first beach huts around the same period, c1900.

Sandbanks

246, 247 In 1896 the 'Queen' magazine published an article on 'The Haven Hotel, Parkstone-on-Sea.' It read: 'Many folk know Bournemouth, and probably as many more are familiar with Poole Harbour and its artistic surroundings, but very few know a small tongue of land jutting straight out into the sea between these two townships. It is only a narrow strip, so narrow that in winter the waves dash up on either side and almost wash away the sandhills and the road; but gorse struggles to grow among the snow-white silvery sand, and here and there a tuft of heather, intersected by the long swaying grass which is to be found on almost every shore. A mile along this wave-washed shore a few coastguard cottages are to be found, one house and the small, but comfortable Haven Hotel. Sandbanks is a fascinating place . . . lonely, wild and healthy.'

The men of Poole sometimes went to camp on Sandbanks for a week-end's shooting. This is one such camp containing representatives of the old Poole families of the Barters and Allens.

Sandbanks

248 Sandbanks had changed little by 1922, the first houses being built on the higher ground.

249 Poole Rowing Club at the Haven, Sandbanks. Many members of the Poole Rowing Club had gone by open horse carriages to meet the eight oarsmen of the Rowing Club. A driver, complete with top hat, awaits their return. On the left of the group, next to the Coastguard, are Dolph Shutler, the President, and Frank Bacon, two of the main traders of High Street.

250 The Coastguard Look-out & Haven Hotel, 1913. Marconi's mast, from which he sent the first wireless message to the Isle of Wight in 1896 is seen to the left. The wreck shown on the right was the remains of the Harbour Board's dredger, the *Pioneer*, placed there in 1910 to form a breakwater.

252 Harbour View House, Tea Rooms and Recreation Ground. Harbour View House was built by Mr Harvey to accommodate visitors to Sandbanks. The foreshore was let for picnics; teas were provided inside the tearooms.

251 The Sandbanks' Pioneers, Mr and Mrs James Harvey. They bought the coach house and stables which Charles Van Raalte of Brownsea Island had built on the 'smooth side' of Sandbanks near to the Coastguards' cottages, to entitle him to be Mayor of Poole. They developed the site as a recreational centre for boat trips and picnics. His family took over the business when James Harvey retired. He died in 1942, aged 85, and was credited with 'transforming an almost inhabited extremity of Poole into a kind of holiday resort'.

253 A Congregational School Tea-party. Mr. Harvey's grounds became a popular venue for Sunday School outings and other gatherings. Parties would go there either by horse-drawn charabangs or by Harvey's boats from Poole Quay.

Sandbanks

254 Harvey's Steam Pinnace, 1911. James Harvey was primarily a boatman. He started a regular ferry service between Sandbanks and Shell Bay and North Haven in 1909. It was in this steam pinnace that he took boys from the Hamworthy Boy's Brigade and boys from Eton and Harrow to Brownsea to form the first Boy Scouts' Camp.

255 Lady Baden Powell in one of Harvey's boats about to visit Brownsea. Lady Baden Powell had lived in Parkstone prior to her marriage at St Peter's Church, Parkstone and it was here her son was later christened.

256 *Ferry Nymph* with Charles and Jim Harvey. After the Second World War *Ferry Nymph* proudly exhibited her brass plate commemorating her exploits at Dunkirk. Harvey's *Southern Queen,* and *Island Queen,* one of the boats of Tom Davis, Harvey's competitor on the Haven Ferry, were not so lucky. They were both sunk off Dunkirk.

257 Harvey's *Ferry Naiad* with a very full load of happy picnickers at Sandbanks.

258 Sandbanks in the 1920's was being developed. Houseboats had been anchored off-shore in the harbour. Mr Henry Burden Junr. was the first to do this. He converted an old RNLI lifeboat into a houseboat and anchored it there in 1912. Others followed his example until in 1930 the Harbour Board ordered their removal. Many were moved to the Harbour side of Shell Bay.

259 The groynes shown in the photograph were built at Sandbanks following the consultant's report of 1891 in which he expressed fear that a heavy south-west gale might cause a breach in Sandbanks with dire consequences to the harbour channel. By 1895 he was able to report that the groynes 'had answered far beyond his expectation'. The groynes collected so much sand that they became submerged.

260 The Competing ferries. Tom Davis's boats are still competing successfully with the chain ferry. In June 1927 the Bournemouth-Swanage Motor Road and Ferry Co. had sought an injunction in the High Court to stop Harveys and Tom Davis from ferrying passengers between Sandbanks and South Haven. The Corporation supported the ferrymen and authorised the Mayor to give evidence in their support and they won the case.

The Haven Passage Ferry was the last of Poole Harbour's many ferries over the harbour to survive.

Sandbanks

261 Sandbanks as seen from Brownsea Island, 1950.

262 The Beach, Sandbanks, 1946. The impediments of war took much longer to clear away than it had taken to install in the heady days of 1940 when the Germans had been expected almost immediately. Sandbanks had been converted into a military stronghold in the war. The five hundred residents were all issued with special passes. Entry to the peninsula was otherwise prohibited.

263 Poole Bay, 1946, with some of the beach defences still intact.

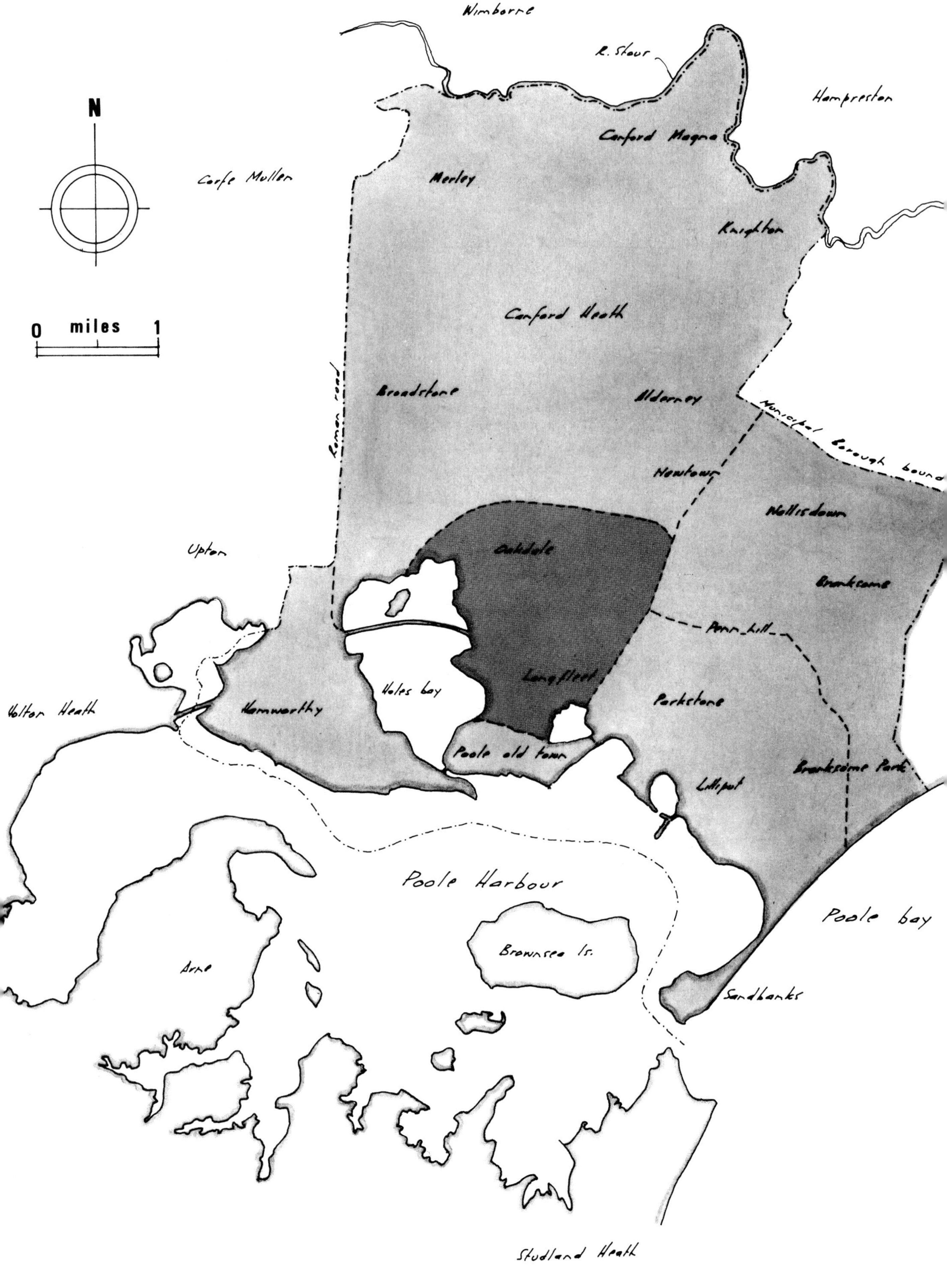

Longfleet

Longfleet, 'a place where the river ebbs and flows', takes its name from the waters of Holes bay which comprises its western boundary. From the end of Holes Bay its boundary turns in a wide sweep across the south part of Canford Heath to Constitution Hill from which it ran in a straight line towards what was the extremity of Parkstone Bay, now Poole Park.

Longfleet was ideally placed for its farmers to supply the town. For centuries it was composed of open ground of the 'wastes' of the manor and numerous farms whose tenants paid their tithes towards the support of the Church of St James.

For centuries there was little incentive for Poole residents to move out of the Old Town unless they wished to farm the land. High Street ended with a style and a footpath and travel was difficult from the Town Gate until the Turnpike Roads were laid down. Moreover, there was plenty of spare ground within the town which had not been developed before the 19th century.

But the position changed with the population explosion which came to Poole after the Napoleonic Wars ended in 1815. In the following ten years all the spare ground of the town had been used, old stables had been converted into cottages, larger houses had been divided and cottages occupied many of the back gardens of even the meanest of houses. By that time there was not only no more room in the Old Town but there was a positive incentive for those who could afford it to move out into the healthier environment of Longfleet, and villas started to appear in Longfleet.

This gradual development of the area just outside the town boundaries continued. In 1833 the lord of the manor encouraged the development further by providing the money for the building of St Mary's Church on Longfleet Hill and, six years later, for a National School to be built nearby. This development had been helped, by the building of two turnpike roads leading to Wimborne and Ringwood from Poole. The workhouse, too, was erected in Longfleet when the Poor Law Commissioners created the Poole Union of parishes. The Union Workhouse was built in a street then called Union Street but later renamed St Mary's Road.

But, despite this early impetus, Longfleet developed only slowly and mainly round its common boundary with Poole in Parkstone Road, Wimborne Road, Serpentine Road and Seldown. Even as late as 1881 its population was only 2406 (of whom 138 were officers and inmates of the workhouse) and it only increased by 344 in the following ten years.

By this time, though, the stile at the top of High Street had long been a thing of the past. High Street had been extended into Longfleet and shops and offices had been built along part of the road. It had its Railway Hotel in Towngate Street and its Temperance Hotel (the present Dolphin) in what was then known as Station Road.

But by far the greater part of Longfleet's 1289 acres was still taken up by farmland. In 1890 there were still twelve farms there, ranging from Bushel Mill Farm and Milestone Farm on its perimeter to farms at Stanley Green, Oakdale and Tatnam nearer to the Old Town boundary.

It was, though, in this year that part of the farmland bordering the Parkstone Road was taken over by the Corporation for the construction of Poole Park and, a few years later, the move of the Cornelia Hospital from Market Street into the cleaner air of Longfleet, gave further impetus to its development. By 1897 it was obviously recognised that Longfleet was going to develop strongly for in 1897 the National School there, first erected in 1839 was extended to accommodate 250 boys, 190 girls and 230 infants even though the average attendance at the school was only 299.

264 High Street in 1870, showing its extension into Longfleet. At first there were few shops. On the left was the building used to provide Poole's first cinema. Lower down the street, behind the fence was the site of the Longfleet Rope Works which stretched back into what became known as Ladies Walking Field after the habit of the women walking to weave the ropes round the upright poles there. Later the ropework's building became the White House Laundry in front of which Kingland Crescent was built during the Second World War.

265 Topp's Corner, Longfleet. Topp's Grocery Store and his adjoining tavern had been built on what was known as Cutler's meadow where, according to Poole legend, Mary Cutler had been hanged for the murder of her child despite being promised a reprieve if she tended to the victims of the plague. The Topp family were butchers in Poole for many generations.

266 High Street in 1874 showing the Toll House at the beginning of Wimborne Road. Shop fronts were later built out from the houses on the left to the line of the front railings.

267 Longfleet in 1880. Few shops had yet appeared there.

268 The tram terminus, Station Road, Longfleet, 1902. The Liberal Central Office for Poole is on the left. The road was later incorporated as part of Towngate Street.

269 Park Road about 1900. Park-keepers' lodges were built at each of the two main entrances to the Park. Park Road was later extended to the right towards the railway at the side of the park lake and houses built there facing the lake. The Corporation also built its open air swimming bath near the railway. It was used each summer until recent times.

270 The Allotments between Kingland Road and the park lake. Some of the land was later incorporated in the playing fields for the Poole Grammar School, the buildings and grounds of which were taken over by Seldown School when the Grammar School moved to its new premises off Gravel Hill. Many of the allotments, however, remained in use.

271 Parkstone Road, 1874. St Joseph's Convent is on the left of the photograph on the corner of Churchfield Road. The track on the right became Mount Pleasant Road and overlooked land which was later bought by the Corporation for incorporation in Poole Park.

272 The Old Farm, Parkstone Road, 1875. A view over the harbour from the back of St Mary's Churchyard showing the Old Farm then occupying the land between Parkstone Road and Parkstone Bay.

273 St Joseph's Convent, 1875. A view from the same place as 272 but looking back towards St Joseph's Convent and Poole.

274 The junction of the two roads leading to Wimborne and Ringwood in about 1890. Toll gates were originally across the road but had been removed in 1867.

275 'The Round House', the toll house which stood at the entrance to the town in the open space in front of the original George Hotel. After it ceased to be used as a toll house it was used as a newsagent's shop from which, to the horror of many local people, newspapers were sold on Sundays as well as throughout the week. It was demolished in 1926.

276 The 'Drum Druid' junction of Longfleet Road and Parkstone Road, 1926. On the demolition of the Round House and the George Hotel in about 1926 the bronze water fountain was placed on the Round House site.

277 Longfleet Hill, c1880. Subsequent development along the escarpment of Longfleet Hill tended to obscure the church and subdue the hill.

278 Longfleet Hill, 1904. A view of Longfleet Hill from Poole Park shows development starting along the ridge of Longfleet Hill.

279 Greenfield Cottages, Kingland Place, 1929. Up to the turn of the century Kingland Road was a little track only 14 feet wide despite there being a number of villas and a row of cottages along it and in Seldown Lane.

280 'Seacroft' and 'Belvedere', Kingland Place, 1960. After the demolition of Greenfield Cottages Kingland Road had been widened. When Kingland Crescent was built in 1943 it was first suggested that it should be named Poole Circus. Members of the Council did not like the suggested name. Meanwhile the *Poole Herald* took a poll of its readers to find out what would be the popular choice of names. 37% of them voted for 'Poole Central'; 22% for 'Kingsway'; 17% for Kingland Crescent and 12% for 'Terminus Way'. Later 9 members of the Council voted for 'Kingland Crescent' and 8 for 'Kingsway'.

281 The junction of Kingland Road with High Street, 1960. Burden's Grocery Store is on the corner with High Street. All these properties were bought by the Corporation for the construction of the new shopping centre. The Arndale Development Co. won the competition to be the developers and managers of the centre. Mr Chippindale, its general manager, suggested that the centre should be named the 'Kingdale Centre' but few were enthusiastic to adopt this name and it was left to be called after the name of the developing company which itself had been a composite of parts of the names of the two directors, Mr Argenback and Mr Chippindale. They applied this name to a number of other shopping centres built by the company later.

282 Longfleet shops, 1934, at the time when the tramways were about to be superseded by the Hants and Dorset Motor Services who then already ran services in Lower Parkstone and from Longfleet to neighbouring towns in Dorset and Hampshire.

283 Burden's Grocery Store and C T Snooks' Longfleet Post Office, 1960. The principal gas main from the Pitwines Gasworks was laid under the railway and through Longfleet Place between these two shops. A large reinforced concrete tunnel had to be built round it to ensure the safety of Marks & Spencer's store when the Arndale Centre was built. A few years later gas ceased to be made at Pitwines.

284 The Longfleet shops in their heyday, in about 1930.

285 Wimborne Road, 1895, near the site of the present Fire Brigade Station. These massive steam rollers were for long a feature of road repairs to consolidate the gravelled surface after it had been disturbed.

286 Garland Road, Longfleet. The old thatched cottage, later the site of the Derby and Joan Club built there in 1953. Garland Road was named after the Old Poole merchants of that name. The adjoining road was named after the Lester family but was later renamed Jolliffe Road (after another family of Poole merchants) presumably for fear that Lester Road would be confused with Leicester Road.

287 The Municipal Buildings were built in 1932 near the junction of Longfleet and Parkstone on land which had been at the extremity of Parkstone Bay. The photograph shows the building prior to its forecourt being taken up by car parking and the erection of the other civic buildings on the land nearby.

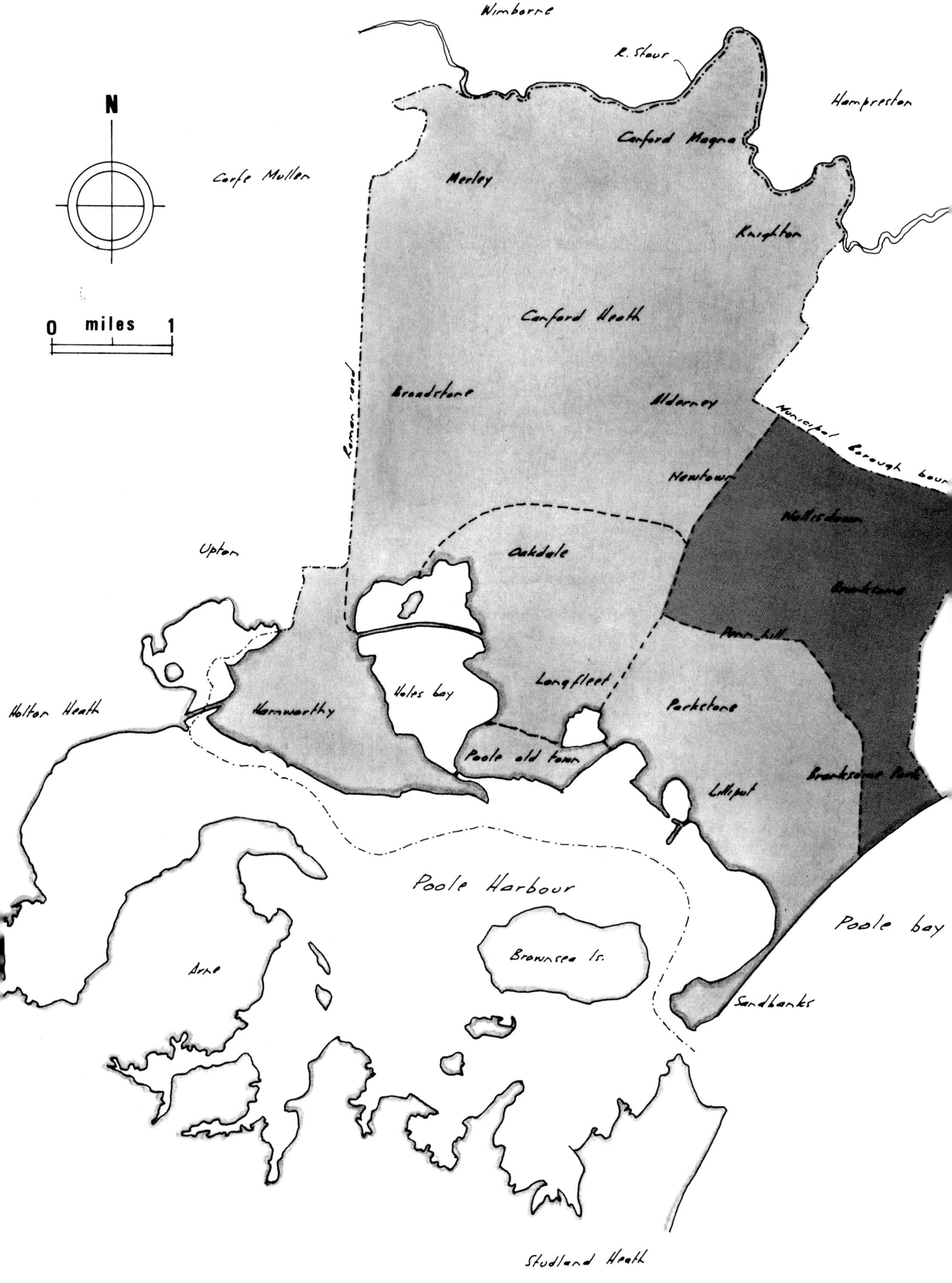

Branksome

The greater part of Branksome lies between the range of hills along which Wallisdown Road has been built on the north and Ashley Road on the south but, in addition, Branksome has an area facing the sea as its south-western boundary sweeps south at the end of Ashley Road to the cliffs at Martello Park.

The whole of the land was for centuries open heathland, part of the wastes of the manor of Canford. Most of it was hilly and of little agricultural value. At first it was only used by the lord of the manor and his friends for shooting over and to a limited extent by the population for pasture or turbary. Later, the level ground between the two range of hills was sometimes used for occasional games and became known as 'Playfields' and as the site for camps for the local Territorials.

The development of Branksome was slow and patchy. Most of its early development took place near its common boundary with Parkstone, north of Ashley Road. It was here that the Poole Corporation had been allotted a considerable area of ground as part of its compensation for the loss of common rights over the rest of the wastes of the manor. It was many years before the Corporation could make any use of the land but, about a hundred years ago, it was able to let off building plots on 99-year leases to builders for housing development, albeit at nominal rents. It was, therefore, in this area, just north of Ashley Road where the Branksome Urban District Council built its offices, its depot and eventually its Public Library.

Its eastern boundary after running just north of Ashley Road turned south near Pottery Junction and a few shops, the Branksome Railway Hotel and its station were in the Branksome area before the boundary ran south to the sea.

It was this southern area of Branksome whose development made its name famous. At first it was an area occupied only by a solitary house, Branksome Tower, which was said to have existed from the middle of the 17th century and was built on the cliffs between Branksome Chine and Branksone Dene Chine. In 1860 an approach road was built from the main Bournemouth road to the house. It was nearly a mile long, all within the parklands of the house. A lodge was built at the entrance just within the Branksome and Dorset boundary with that of Bournemouth and Hampshire and, because of this, the junction of the roads became known as County Gates.

It was only later that the grounds of the house were developed as a high-class residential estate which became known as Branksome Park and covenants were imposed on all purchasers for the benefit of Branksome Tower that no house built on the estate should occupy less than an acre of ground. The estate and the mansion, converted into the Branksome Tower Hotel, made this area of Branksome famous. The land surrounding the Branksome stream was given to the Corporation to form a woodland walk which stretches the whole length of the estate to the sea and, though blocks of flats have now taken the place of many of the old mansions in and around The Avenue, the area has retained its high-class residential nature and the walk through the woodlands surrounding the Branksome stream still retains its character despite most of its water and its two lakes having disappeared. The two Chines, too, have been acquired by the Corporation as well as the foreshore in front of the Branksome Tower Hotel and form a popular seaside area. Meanwhile the Branksome Tower Hotel has itself been demolished to give place for further residential development.

288 The Dorset Militia Camp at Playfields, 1877. At this time the large open spaces of Branksome were ideal for military camps and training.

Dorset Militia Camp at Playfields near Poole 1877.

289 Visitors to the Dorset Rifle Volunteers' Camp in 1879. Mr J B Durell, standing second from the left in the photograph, was the father of Mr John Durell whose death at 'Blenheim' in Mount Pleasant Road in 1936 brought a family connection with Poole which had lasted over 500 years to an end. Standing next to him is Mr A K Witt.

290 Looking down Alder Road after a snow storm in 1925. There was still little development in this area.

291 Looking north into Cranbrook Road in the 1930's shows development proceeding from Ashley Road.

292 Cranbrook Road, 1934. Looking down the still undeveloped northern part of Cranbrook Road. A photograph taken by the Bus Company when considering its services when taking over the public transport in Poole.

293 A picture postcard of the 1920's showing County Gates, the boundary of the towns of Bournemouth and Poole and the Counties of Hampshire and Dorset with an old open-topped tramcar.

294 The lodge at the entrance to the old accommodation roadway to Branksome Tower, now part of the office site of the Frizzell Group of Insurance Companies.

295 The Avenue looking north from its junction with Dalkeith Road in 1958. Prior to the development of the Branksome Park Estate the land to the left of the photograph had been a clearing known as 'Buttercup Field' which had been a favourite resort for the residents of Parkstone and Branksome and for picnic parties.

296 The Lower Lake, like the higher one, fed by the stream which ran through the western side of the Branksome Park estate. The trustees of the Bury estate gave the Corporation 40 acres of land bordering the stream, which was laid out as an amenity area. Most of the water of the stream, however, was lost and only a small part of this lake was left when the Corporation took it over. In enclosing this small lake the Corporation designed the concrete retaining wall to represent the south coast of England.

297, 298 Branksome Chine formed one of the easier accesses to the sands and sea along the coast of Poole but it was not extensively used before the car became in common use and the frontage was developed by beach huts along the line of the cliffs.

299 Branksome Tower was for long a single towered private residence. The Avenue, Branksome Park, was built in 1860 as an approach road to it. The Hayden family owned it for many years and it became famous as an hotel. In recent years it was bought by property developers who demolished the hotel. Its site has recently been redeveloped as a housing estate.

300 The grounds of the hotel included the cliffs and foreshore fronting the sea. They were conveyed to the Corporation when sea defence works were constructed along the hotel's frontage.

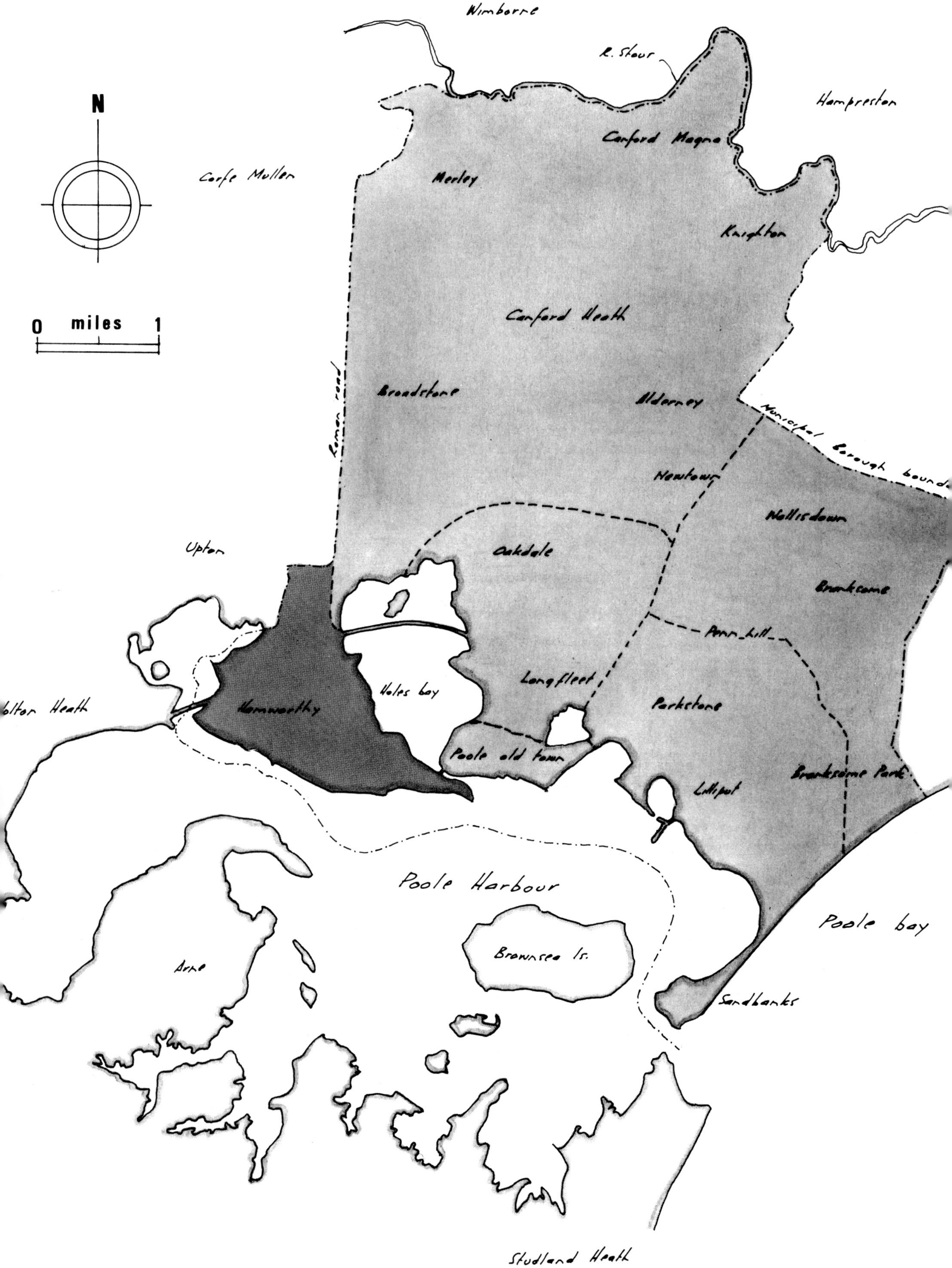

Hamworthy

Hamworthy, 'a hamlet between two waters', was the earliest part of present-day Poole to be settled. It was the 'Moriconium' of the Romans, a village settlement, convenient for their trade, near deep water and the terminus of a system of well-constructed roads which led from the Hamworthy quayside northwards round Holes Bay to Corfe Mullen and Badbury Rings where it joined the Via Iceniana, the road which ran between Old Sarum and Dorchester. It is still this road which forms the illogical boundary between Broadstone and Corfe Mullen.

Originally there were two small manors in Hamworthy, High Ham situate round the neighbourhood of the Church and the old Rectory (and owned for many years by the Turbervilles of Bere Regis) and Lower or South Ham which was bought by the lord of the manor of Canford before Queen Elizabeth's reign.

Old Poole had little to do with Hamworthy prior to the building of the bridge between the quays and the construction of the turnpike road from the Hamworthy side of the bridge to Upton crossroads except for a small area opposite Poole Quay on which the Poole shipyards were established and an area of scrubland known as 'Maidens' Walk' to which the women of the town were ferried in Tudor and Stuart times where, it was reported, 'they daily hang and spread their linen clothes to dry them in winter and summer'.

Despite this, Hamworthy figured largely in Poole's history when it sided with the Roundheads in the Civil Wars despite the rest of Dorset being on the Royalist side. Fortifications were then built near the present Rigler Road to defend the quays against any attack from the west. At that time, too, Hamworthy lost its first chapel when it was pulled down by Cromwell's soldiers, then quartered in the old manor house, for its stone to be used to reinforce Poole's town wall and to build a magazine at the Town Gate. According to Hamworthy legend Cromwell himself visited his headquarters at the Manor House and stayed the night there. Its second floor was used as a hospital for his wounded soldiers and the large mound nearby in the churchyard was said to be the burying place of the soldiers killed in the fighting.

Whatever the truth of these traditional stories, it was certainly true that it was soldiers from his Hamworthy garrison who unsuccessfully invested Corfe Castle in 1643. The castle, defended by Lady Bankes and a few retainers, defied all attempts to take it until, two years later, it was taken by treachery. Following this, Parliament decided that the castle should be 'slighted', a task which was only too well executed. The troops took several months in early 1646 to make sure that the castle could never again be effectively defended.

When Hamworthy was eventually brought firmly into the Poole ambit by the building of the first bridge its population was only 308, but the lord of the manor then anticipated an increase in population and it was he who built the old St Michael's church and gave the manor house to the church for use as a rectory. Hamworthy was added to the Poole Borough by the Boundary Act, 1833.

Hamworthy Bridges

301 'Hamworthy Bridge' in 1880, a few years before it was replaced. It was built by the Bridge Company, sponsored by W F S Ponsonby, the lord of the manor, despite the opposition of the Poole Corporation who, after once deciding that the bridge 'would be a great convenience to the town' then reversed the decision when it was found that the lord of the manor himself intended to build a toll bridge. It then opposed the passing of the Act of Parliament giving him these powers on the ground that it would impede the scour of the receding tide from Holes Bay on the quays and congest the narrow streets of the town by encouraging through-traffic to the west coming through the town.

302 The Second Bridge in 1885. Even in 1867 the condition of the old bridge caused public complaint. The small opening which could be made for sea traffic often caused damage to ships' bowsprits; waggons over three tons were banned and, it was said, the bridge 'squeaked, shrieked and creaked from summit to base' whenever a waggon went over it. It was replaced by this iron bridge in 1885. Two years after it was built the Corporation refused Lord Wimborne's offer to sell it for £8,000, but in 1919 made a compulsory purchase order to buy it. In 1922 a price had still not been agreed and the matter was sent to arbitration where a price of £15,914 was fixed, plus costs of £1,888.

303 'Poole Bridge', 1927. Having completed their purchase of the old bridge it was found that it required so much renewal and repair that it was prudent to build a new one. It was completed in 1927 at a cost of £33,591. Lord Shaftesbury was thrown from his horse a day or two before he was due to open the bridge and it was opened by the then Mayor, Ald. Herbert Carter.

304 The first Hamworthy Church. After the 'fanatics' had pulled down Hamworthy's original chapel in 1649, Hamworthy had to wait for 176 years for a new one. Meanwhile it had remained a 'chapelry, tithing or hamlet in the Parish of Sturminster Marshall'. This church of St Michael was built in 1825/6 by W F S Ponsonby. It was demolished on the building of the new church in 1964.

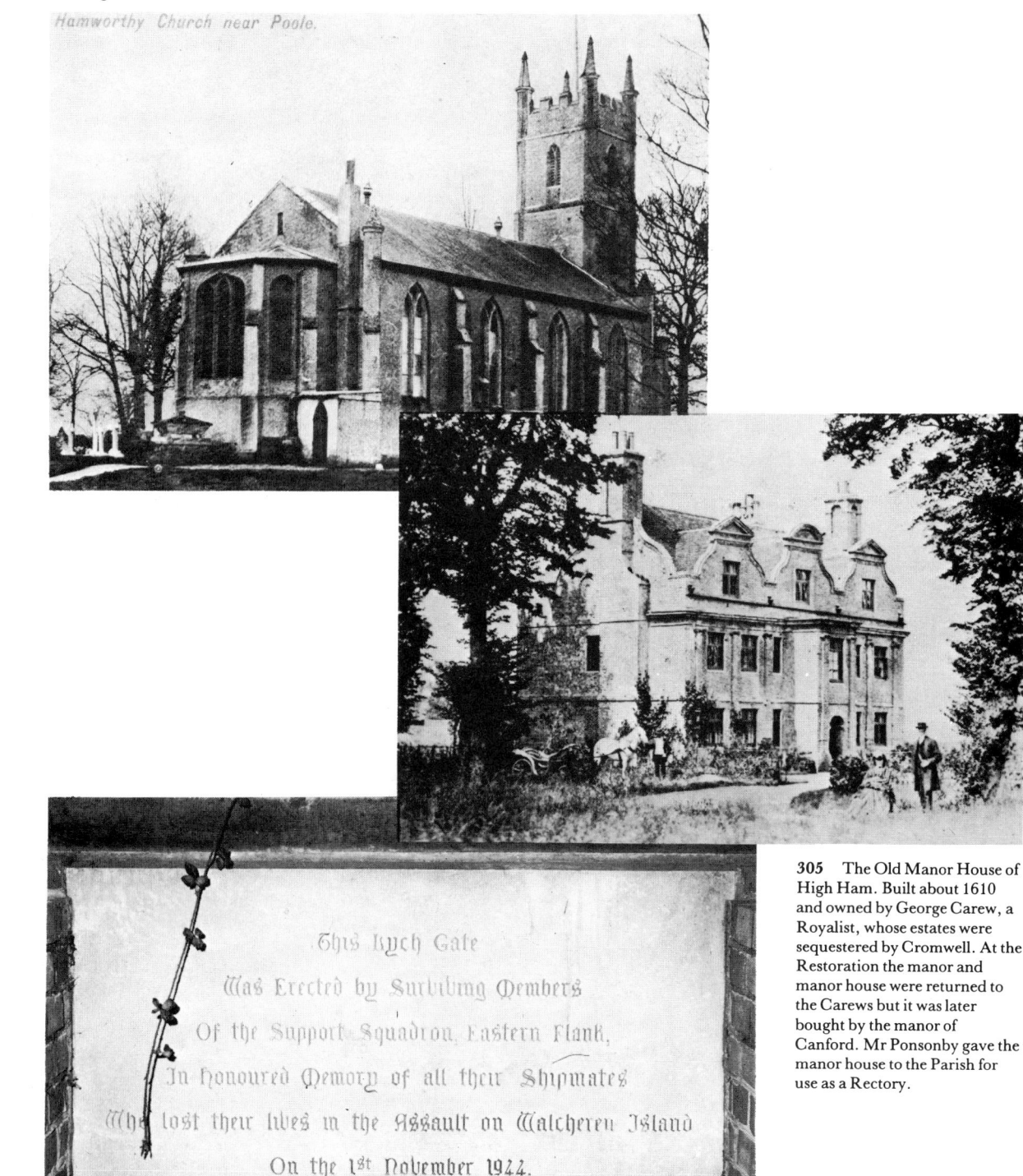

305 The Old Manor House of High Ham. Built about 1610 and owned by George Carew, a Royalist, whose estates were sequestered by Cromwell. At the Restoration the manor and manor house were returned to the Carews but it was later bought by the manor of Canford. Mr Ponsonby gave the manor house to the Parish for use as a Rectory.

306 The plaque on the Lych Gate, St Michael's. The Lych Gate was erected by the surviving marines of HMS Turtle, Hamworthy, in memory of their comrades who fell in their attack on the island of Walcheren at the mouth of the Scheldt. The seaward attack had been made by twenty-five craft of the Support Squadron stationed at Hamworthy. Although it succeeded in its objective of opening the port of Antwerp and allowing the Allies to advance on Germany, nine of their craft were sunk and another nine crippled by the German shore batteries.

307 An Empire Flying Boat at Hamworthy in 1946. BOAC was formed at the beginning of the last war and its flying boats were moved from Southampton to Poole in 1939. Throughout the war and for some years afterwards BOAC headquarters was housed at the Poole Harbour Yacht Club premises and its flying boats flew from Poole to the Near East, the Far East and Australia and America. It was from Poole Harbour that the first British passenger flight across the north Atlantic was made, setting out from Poole Harbour on 3 August, 1940.

To the left of the flying boat is an abandonned landing craft from the Normandy invasion.

The 'hard' on which the flying boat is standing was originally built for the Sunderland flying boats of RAF Station Hamworthy used in the war for submarine patrols over the Western Approaches.

308 Sydenham's Timber Pond, Hamworthy. Sydenhams was the largest Poole timber yard, but other timber yards such as J J Norton's and May & Hassel had similar ponds in the harbour. The logs were barked and then put in the pond to season. Stakes were driven into the mud to contain the logs.

309 Hamworthy School in 1905 was then on the outskirts of the development as Hamworthy grew out from the bridge.

310 Hamworthy Junction at the end of the 19th century. The station was on the road to the left where the line into Hamworthy branched off the main line between Wimborne and Dorchester. The road shown going straight on under the railway bridge was the old turnpike road from the bridge to Upton Cross and Blandford, now Blandford Road.

311 The Hamworthy Junction Hotel. An hotel inevitably appeared soon after any station was built.

312 Hamworthy Boy Scouts Troop, 1909. The Boy Scouts Association was formed in 1908. It was only appropriate that one of the early troops to be formed should be the Hamworthy Troop as one-third of the boys on the original Brownsea Island camp were boys from Hamworthy.

313 The Red Lion Hotel, 1900. Like many Dorset towns Hamworthy had its Red Lion Hotel.

164

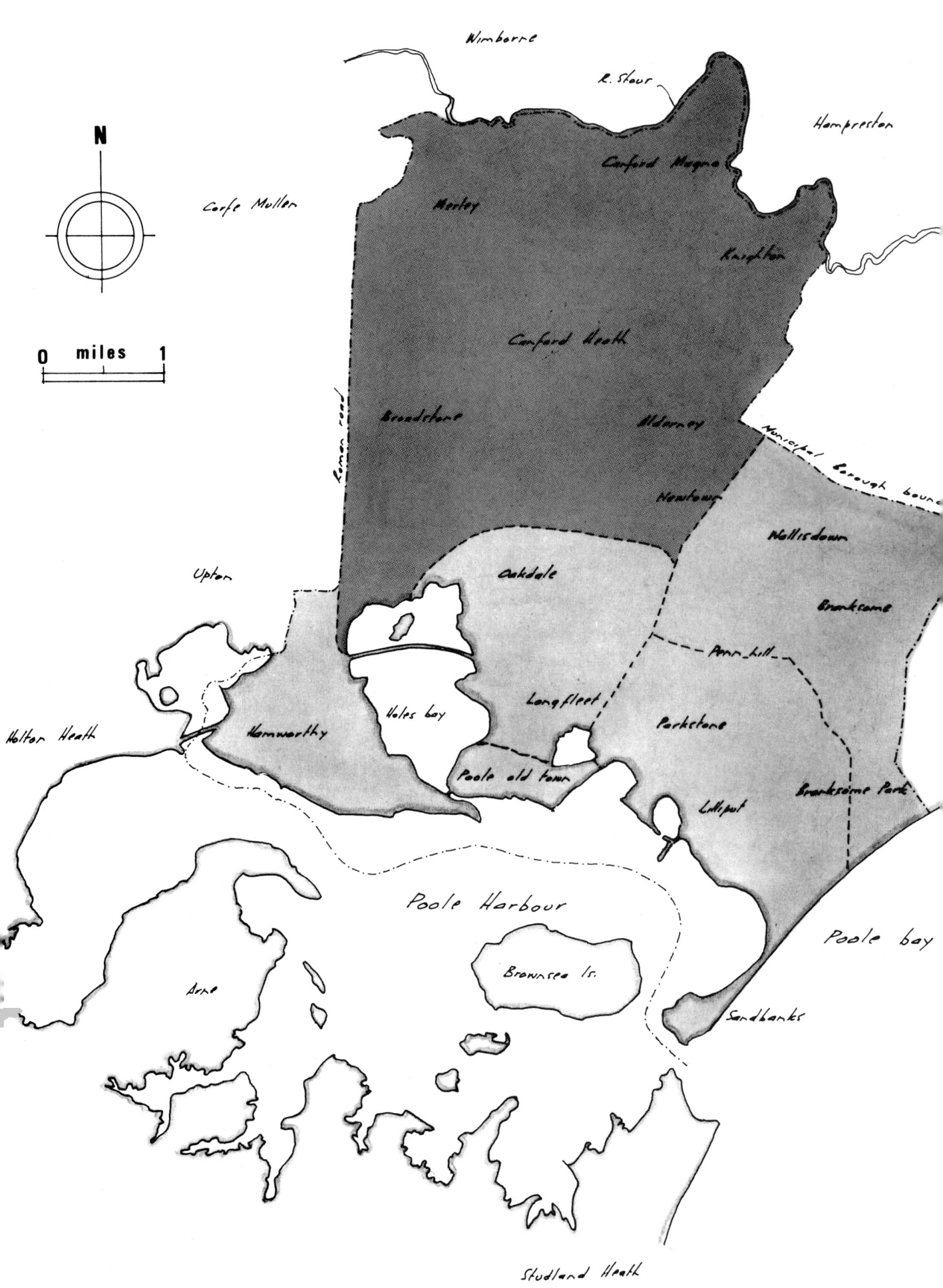

Broadstone

Despite the turnpike road from Gravel Hill to Blandford having run through the Corfe Hills for nearly a century, the area was virtually uninhabited in 1845, when the South Western Railway Company was planning its main line between Wimborne and Dorchester. There was therefore no question then of building a station on the line before it reached the outskirts of Hamworthy where a Junction station could be built for a branch line to Poole to come to the Hamworthy side of the Quay bridge.

In 1872, however, the railway decided it needed a direct line into Poole with a 'New Poole' station for passengers and goods. Such a branch line would have to leave the main line nearer to Wimborne so that it could run down the eastern side of Holes Bay. It was decided that the appropriate place to branch off the main line would be near the juncture of the main line with the Blandford turnpike road. It was here, therefore, that they built their new station and, as it was to run to the 'New Poole' station, it was logical that it should be called 'New Poole Junction'.

It was the existence of the railway station at the side of Blandford Road which was to give impetus to the development of Broadstone as well as to give it its name.

The name of the village gradually evolved from the confusion which its first name of 'New Poole Junction' caused with the 'New Poole' station in Longfleet. The Company was at a loss how to resolve the difficulty. Four years after the opening of the station they added the name of the adjoining farm to its name and called it 'New Poole Junction and Broadstone' and, when this did little to lessen the confusion, they changed the names round and called it 'Broadstone and New Poole Junction'. Local people now took a hand in it. The area was becoming to be known as Broadstone and Mr Waterman, the owner of the farm, had no objection to the station being called simply 'Broadstone'. He would even change the name of his farm to obviate any further confusion. Finally, in 1890, the railway at last agreed. They changed the name of its station to 'Broadstone' and Mr Waterman renamed his farm 'Brookside' and the area had its own separate identity even though officially still part of the village and parish of Canford Magna.

Four years later the area was amalgamated with Kinson, Lytchett Minster and Lytchett Matravers into a new Rural District Council called the Poole Rural District Council.

Broadstone was then approaching the stage when it might claim to be a village in its own right. In 1888 five villas had been built facing the main road between Ridgeway and Macaulay Road; the church, parsonage and three pairs of villas built nearby and the Railway Hotel in 1890. In 1893 Mr Watkins had opened his store and off-licence on the corner of York Road and his in-laws had retired to the house on the opposite corner. A further two shops with a doctor's surgery had also come to Broadstone. These developments with the older buildings, the Manor House in Station Road; Audlem Lodge and Eli Sharland's The Pines in Ridgeway with his brickworkers' cottages nearby and Louise French's grocery store and post office between Macaulay Road and Station Road plus the school built by Lord Wimborne, gave a solid foundation on which the village could be built.

In 1898 Lord Wimborne had his golf course laid out and offered plots for sale nearby which were gradually taken up by retired couples or by more wealthy people who wanted a second home, and Broadstone was palpably growing.

By 1906 Broadstone was finally recognised as a separate village from Canford and a Broadstone Parish Council was formed with Lord Wimborne as its Chairman. It had at last established its own separate identity which, despite all the changes and development which has since taken place, it has always retained.

In 1933, however, when its population was still only 2,500 its residents were suddenly called upon to decide where their destiny lay. In 1931 Kinson had been taken out of the Poole Rural District to be incorporated in Bournemouth and the remnants of the Rural District were not strong enough to exist on their own. Broadstone and Canford had a choice. They could ask to become part of a new Rural District Council, they could apply to become part of the Wimborne and Cranborne R D C or they could opt to join Poole. They finally decided to join Poole and, in 1933, the 6,000 acres of Broadstone and Canford became part of the Borough of Poole.

314 Broadstone School c 1890. William Wheeler was appointed headmaster in 1888 and remained there till his retirement in 1925. For many years he managed Lord Wimborne's golf course and was the Chairman of the Broadstone Parish Council for the last ten years of its existence before its amalgamation with Poole.

315 Eli Sharland's brickworks, c 1880. 'Granfer' Sharland lived at 'The Pines', Ridgeway, overlooking his brickworks and at this time the road running up into Broadstone from Poole was known as 'Sharland's Hill'. The site of the brickworks now forms part of the Broadstone Recreation Ground.

316 From the water tower in 1923. The five and a half acres of ground given to the village by Miss Kennedy being laid out as a Recreation Ground. Lord Wimborne gave the rest of the land which was incorporated into the Recreation Ground.

317 Broadstone Scholars with their teachers, 1905. Miss Pike
two to her left, were long remembered by their scholars. The ca
Pond as well as Creekmoor. The scholars in the photograph pro
First World War.

n the left in the back row, and William Wheeler, headmaster,
f the school, included the little village of Waterloo round Hatch
d all the forty-four men of Broadstone who lost their lives in the

318 Rose Farm, 1905. One of the little farmsteads of Broadstone. It stood on the site of the present children's playground. Springdale Road was built across the hill on the far side of the photograph. It lead from Higher Blandford Road and was eventually extended to join the Old Wareham Road in Corfe Mullen.

319 Broadstone village, c 1906. The railway trucks on the far left are about to enter Broadstone station. The Railway Hotel and the Lavender factory are shown just ahead of the train.
Charles Rivers-Hill, who farmed Corfe Lodge Farm, had turned over 60 acres of his farm to the cultivation of lavender in partnership with Mr. Tollemach. The two crops of lavender each year were distilled and then bottled at this factory in Station Road. Many women were employed there in weaving the wicker coverings to the white china bottles – later changed to dark green bottles covered with open-work raffia. For 20 years the business thrived and, during this period, Broadstone was often referred to as 'The Lavender Village'.

320 'Broadstone and New Poole Junction', 1887. The Station name plate of 'New Poole Junction' has had the name 'Broadstone' added to the top of it. The loop line to the right led to Poole station. The other line was the main line between Wimborne and Dorchester.

321 Station Road, Broadstone. The old Manor House on the right of the photograph is now the offices of Harry J Palmer (Broadstone) Ltd. The building at the end of the road is the Railway Hotel. Just in front of it is the Lavender Factory which was bought in 1924 by Mr. A B ('Fred') Haynes who had established a chemist's shop next door to it. He converted the old factory building into a hall and headquarters for his Broadstone Athletic Club. The building was destroyed by fire in 1935 and was replaced by Nissen huts for the Athletic Club.

322 Broadstone's First Shop. Louise French's house, the first shop in Broadstone which also became Broadstone's first post office. It was on the corner of Blandford Road and Station Road.

323 Mr. E Watkins opened his grocery and off-licence shop in 1893. It is the building on the left of the photograph, taken from York Road. Mrs. Watkins's father and mother, Mr. and Mrs. Frank Bailey retired from Milestone Farm which lay opposite New Inn at Oakdale to live in the house on the right of the photograph. Mr. Bailey was killed on Broadstone station in 1899 and Mrs. Bailey let her front room to the Wilts & Dorset Bank. Lloyds Bank afterwards took over the Wilts & Dorset Bank and eventually the whole of Mrs. Bailey's house which still forms their Broadstone branch office.

324 Broadstone's Jubilee Bonfire, 1897. The photograph shows only the base of the enormous bonfire made by the few residents of Broadstone to commemorate Queen Victoria's Jubilee. It was built on the hill at Widworthy on farmer Venner's land. Mr. Venner is standing on the left of the photograph. To his left is Mr. Walter Scutt (whose business in West Quay Road was later amalgamated with that of Christopher Hill) then Mr. Atkins, Mr. Rawlins, Mr. William Wheeler, Mr. Louise French, the Rev. Long-Schreiber and Mr. Gilbert Clark. Mr. Waterman is on the left of the front row and Mr. William Lawford and Mr. Coombes are to his left. Mr. Watkins is on the right with one of Mr. Wheeler's sons.

325 Broadstone Golf Pavilion, 1906. The Golf Club House became quite a centre for Broadstone's social gatherings. On this occasion it was the 'Bazaar and Strawberry Fete' held to raise funds to enlarge the church. The leading ladies of Broadstone all had stalls. Mrs. Weston (hon. secretary), Mrs. Rawlins, Mrs. Wheeler, Mrs. Wilkinson, Mrs. Martin, Mrs. Arnold, Mrs. Besant, Mrs. Purdue and Miss Ford. The fete raised £140 of the £1,400 required for the extension.

Index

Numbers given are page numbers, bold figures indicate illustrations.

Adult School	47
The Age – Mail Coach	89
Alder Road	151
Alexandra, Princess of Wales	50, **50**, 51, 53, 54
Allen Family	129
Almshouses	
St. Georges	31
Roger's	104
Garland's	112
Amity Cinema	46
Amity Hall	**44, 46,** 47
Amity Lodge of Freemasons	**45,** 46
Angel Inn	35, 89
Antelope Hotel	40, 53, 89
Arndale Centre	11, **144, 145**
Arndale Development Co.	144
Arnold, Thomas	8, 9
Arrowsmith, Edward	7
Ashley, Lady Barbara	7
Ashley, Lord	7
Ashley Cross	53, 117, **120**
Ashley Cross, Fire Station	120
Ashley Road	**94, 99,** 149, 151
Avenue, Branksome Park	149, **152,** 154
Avenue Place	101
Bacon & Curtis	42
Baden Powell, Lady Olive	132
Baiter Street (previously Pound Street)	111
Bandstand – Poole Park	57
Barter Family	129
Basset Green – Lifeboat	82
Beaminster Omnibus	44
Beehive Inn	117, **123**
Beech Hurst	49
Belben's Mill Warehouses	**41,** 65
Bell, Thomas	35
Benedetto, 'Papa' – Italian Organ Grinder	115
Bessborough, Earl of	7
Blenheim House	31
Blockships	71
Blue Boar Lane	111
Blue Lagoon	125
Bluebells – Tramcars	91, **94, 95**
Bonham, Christie, Mrs.	86
Bonnett's Store	120
Boundary Commissioners	8
Bournemouth	51, 52, **55,** 89, 90, 91, 118, 149, 166
Bournemouth Queen – Paddle Steamer	84
Bournemouth Silver Band	53
Bowden House	33
Boy Scouts Association	132, **163**
Branksome	89, 149
Branksome Chine	149, **153**
Branksome Dene	51
Branksome Dene Chine	149
Branksome Park, Estate	149, **152, 153**
Branksome Park, Sandbanks and Parkstone Extension Association	90
Branksome Railway Hotel	149
Branksome Tower Hotel	149, **152, 154,** 155
Branksome Urban District Council	91, 149
Bridge	39, **64,** 157, **158,** 159
Brittania Inn	117
Broadstone	**164,** 165, 166, **167, 168-169, 170, 171**
Broadstone Golf Course	11, 173
Broadstone Parish Council	**15,** 165, **166**
Broadstone Post Office	172
Broadstone Recreation Ground	167
Broadstone School	11, **166, 168-169**
Broadstone Station	165, **170, 171**
Brown, Albert ('Alby')	73
Brown, Bill	73
Brown Bottom	90, **96**
Brownsea Castle	**85, 86**
Brownsea Island	11, 75, **85, 86, 87,** 132, **134,** 163
Brownsea Quay	86
Budge, Philip, Mayor of Poole	11, 50, 51, 52, 53, 54, **56**
Bull's Head Inn	**44,** 89
Burden's Grocery Store	**144,** 145
Burgesses of Poole	7, 8
Bury Estate	153
Bus Terminus	39
Butler's Brush Factory	110
Canford Cliffs	**126, 127, 128**
Canford Cliffs Chine	128
Canford Cliffs Hotel	128
Canford Cliffs Road	126
Canford Heath	137
Canford Magna	7, 11, 12, 165
Canford Manor	**6,** 7, 10, 12, **13, 14, 15,** 50, 51, 52
Canford Park	10
Canford School	12
Carriers	89
Carter, Herbert	120, 159
Carter, Owen	102
Castle Hill	117, **119,** 120
Castle Street (previously Fish Street)	70, 101, **106, 107, 108, 109**
Catholic Lane	
See New Street	
Cavendish-Bentinck, George	86, 87
Chapel Lane	53
Charles II	42
Church Street	18, **26, 29, 30,** 32
Churchfield Road	141
Churchill, Lady Cornelia	
See Guest, Lady Cornelia	
Cinnamon Lane	18, **22, 31, 34**
Coastline Company	63
Commercial Road	53, **121**
Congregational Chapel – Parkstone	121
Constitution Hill	90, 91, 118, **118,** 137
Convent of St. Clements	24
Corn Market	**42** 108
Cornelia Working Men's Club	12, **40**
Corporation of Poole	7, 8, 9, 11, 17, 18, 20, 23, 26, 31, 36, 37, 39, 50, 51, 52, 54, 61, 64, 65, 76, 85, 89, 90, 91, 92, 101, 104, 117, 118, 120, 140, 141, 144, 149, 153, 155, 158
Council	
See Corporation of Poole	
County Gates	89, 90, 91, 149, **152**
Court of Record	35
Cranbrook Road	151
Curtis, George	114
Custom House	17, **21,** 60
Cutler, Mary	**138**
Davis, Harry	73
Davis, Tom,	**132, 133**
De Mauley, Lord	
see Ponsonby, Hon. W. F. S.	
Dennetts Lane	**41**
Devonshire, Duchess of	7
Dockers Seat	**114**
Dolphin Brewery	30
Dorchester	8, 157, 165
Dorchester School	119
Dorset House, (Orphanage)	53, **103**
Dorset (Queen's Own) Yeomanry	51, 52
Drum Druid Junction	**142**
Durrell Family	102, **150**
Eagle House	
see Jolliffe House	
Eel Spearing	66
East Quay Road	61, 67
Edward, Prince of Wales (Edward VII)	50, **50,** 51, 52, 53, 54
Edward, Prince of Wales (Edward VIII)	59
Elford, John	, 50, 54
Empire Sentinel – Blockship	71
Embassy – Paddlesteamer	84
Emperor of India – Paddlesteamer	83
Enclosure Acts	7
Etoile – Sailing Ship	81
European Architectural Heritage Year	18
Ferries	
see Ham Ferry	
Sandbanks Ferries	
Ferry Naiad	**132**
Ferry Nymph	**132**
Ferry Steps	64
Fifty-Shilling Tailors	39
Fish Shambles	61, **65**
Fish Street	
see Castle Street	
Fishermen's Depot	**65**
Fishermen's Dock	**68, 69,** 82
Fishermen's Hard	61, 67
Fishing Fleet	67
Fishmarket	65
Flag Head	**126,** 127
Flying Boats	**161**
French, Louise	165, 172, **173**
Friends Meeting House (Lagland Street)	47, **105**
Furzey Island	75
Garland Family	25, **46,** 112, **146**
Garland Road	**146**
Gas Company	63, 68
Gasworks	111, 145
Gee, Rev. W.	**121**
George Inn	
see Scaplen's Court	
George, Prince	51, 52, 54
George Hotel	**142**
Giggers Island	75
Globe Hotel	46

Index

Globe Lane 45
Goathorn 75, **78**
God's Acre
  see St. Mary's Church, Brownsea Island
Gost's Bay
  see Parkstone Bay 117
Gravel Hill 165
Green Island 75
Greenslade, 'Curly' 66
Guest, Lady Charlotte 10, **13**
Guest, Lady Cornelia 11, **15**, 52, 54, **124**
Guest, Freddie 11, **120**
Guest, Sir Ivor Bertie, Lord Wimborne 10, 11, **15**, 50, 51, 54, 120, 165, 167
Guest, Ivor Churchill 12, **51**
Guest, Sir J. J. 10, **13**
Guest, Montague **45**, 51
Guildhall 17, 18, **35**, **36**, 54, 101
Guildhall Tavern (previously Yacht Inn) **33**
Gwatkin, H. F. W. 91, 97, 98

Ham Ferry **64**
Ham Passage House **64**
Hamside **64**
Hamworthy 8, 89, **156**, 157, **158**, **160**, 161, 162, 163
Hamworthy Junction 162
Hamworthy Junction Hotel 162
Hamworthy Manor
  see Rectory, Hamworthy
Hamworthy School 162
Hamworthy Station 93
Handel String Band 54
Handfast Point 77
Harbour 75, 76, **77**, **122**
Harbour Bar 76
Harbour, Map of **74**
Harbour Office 20, 21, 40, 60, 63
Harbour View House 131
Harmer - Lifeboat 82
Harman's Yard 109
Harvey Family **132**, **133**
Harvey, James 131
Haven 130
Haven Cellars
  see Jolliffe House
Haven Hotel **129**, **130**
Hayden Family 154
Hayes, Richard 73
Haynes, A. B. 171
Hermitage 45
High Street 18, 39, **40**, **41**, **42**, **43**, **44**, **45**, **46**, **48**, **49**, 52, 53, 61, **65**, 89, 90, 101, **106**, **107**, **114**, 137, **138**, **139**, **144**, **145**
Hill, Christopher 50
Hill Street **44**, **113**
H.M.S. Flinders - Blockship 71
Hohenlohe, Prince 51, 52, 54
Holes Bay 75, 76, **80**, 101, 137, 157, **158**
'Holly Bank' 53
Hoogstraed, Nuns of 7
Hospitals 11, 12, **45**, 137
Houseboats, in Harbour 133
Hunger Hill 112

The Independent - Mail Coach 89
Italian Winter Garden 86
Ivy House 39, **48**, 110

Jolliffe House (previously Haven Cellars,
  Dorset House and Eagle House) **103**
Jolliffe Family **45**, **103**, **146**

Kennedy, Miss 167
King Charles Inn (previously New Inn) 20, 24
King Street 18, **35**, **104**
Kingland Crescent 39, **138**, **144**
Kingland Place **144**
Kingland Road **144**
King's Hall
  see Town Cellars
King's Head Inn **40**, **41**

Ladies Walking Field 11, 39, 124, **138**
Lady of Avenel - Brigantine 80
Lagland Street 39, 61, 89, **105**
Landing Craft Recovery Unit 71
Lavender Factory, Broadstone **170**, **171**
'Lavender Village' 170
Ledgard, Richard 10
Lester Family **25**, **146**
Levet's Lane 18, 30, 32
Lewen's Iron and Brass Foundry **110**
Liberal Central Office 139
Libraries 12, **40**, **49**, **110**
Lifeboats 82
'Lights in line' 63
Lilliput 117, **125**
London Inn 43
Long Island 75
Longfleet 8, 39, 50, **96**, **99**, **136**, 137, **138**, **139**, 145, 147
Longfleet Bay
  see Holes Bay 101
Longfleet Hill 137, **143**
Longfleet School 11
Looker's Stationers 43
Lower Parkstone 52, **57**, 89, 91, 92
Lytchett Bay 76
Macebearers 37, 52, 53, 91
Manor House, Broadstone 165, **171**
Mansion House (Club) **25**, **26**
Marconi, Guglielmo 130
Market Street 18, **22**, **32**, **33**, **35**, 101
Martello Tower **127**, **128**
Mary Rose - Training Ship 80
Matthews, Henry 66
Matthews, Pat 66
Meadus, Thomas 79
Measurer's Gap 61
Mentone of England 118
Minerva Printing Works 43
Monarch - Paddlesteamer 83
Moriconium 157
Mountaineer - Sloop 79
Municipal Buildings 147
Municipal Elections 8, 9
Municipal Offices, Parkstone 120

National School, Longfleet 137
New Antelope Inn 22
New Inn
  see King Charles Inn
New Orchard 18, **19**, 39, 43, **113**
'New Poole Junction' 165, **170**, **171**
New Quay, Temporary Breakwater 71
New Street (previously Catholic Lane) 17, **22**, **33**, **34**, 101
Newfoundland Dogs 89
Newfoundland Trade 8, **49**, 61, 76, **79**, **80**, 117
North Street 48
Norton, John J. 12, **110**, 161
Notting's Buildings, Lower Parkstone 117

Oakdale 137
Old Bell Inn **109**
Old Farm, Parkstone Road **141**
Old Grey House
  see Canford Manor
Old Greyhound Inn 18, **35**
Old Harry Rocks **77**, **78**, **125**
Old Olster's Stables and Yard **22**, **34**
Old Poole 17, 34, 39, 50, 51, 52, **104**, **111**, 137, 157
Old Town Water Pump 20
Old Town Wall **1**, 52, 53, **56**
Olive, James 46

Paddlesteamers **83**, **84**
Paradise Street **20**, **49**
Park Gates East
  see also Brown Bottom 91, 96
Park Road **140**
Parkstone 8, 50, 51, 89, 117, 118, **119**, **120**, **121**, 122, 147, 149
Parkstone Bay 50, 54, **57**, 101, 117, **121**, 137, **141**, 147
Parkstone Golf Course 11, **124**
Parkstone Hall **120**
Parkstone Park 11, 52, 53, 117, **120**
Parkstone Road 137, **141**, **142**
Parkstone Sailing Club **122**
Parliamentary Elections 7, 8, 10, **36**
Parr, Robert 8, 9
Parrott, 'Capt' George 8, 10
Pavilion, Poole Park 51, 52, 53
Pearce, Robert 37
Pearce, William 119
Penney Family **48**, **70**
Piano and Music Warehouse, High Street **46**
Pillory Street 101
Pioneer - Harbour Board's Dredger 130
Pitwines Gasworks 145
'Playfields' 149, **150**
Polly, Fishing Boat **68**
Ponsonby, Hon. W. F. S. (Lord de Mauley) 7, 8, 9, 126, 158, 160
Ponsonby, Rev. W 126
Poole and District Electric Traction
  Company 89, 90, 91, **94**
Poole Bay 66, 67, **135**
Poole Foundry 119
Poole House 25
Poole, Map of 1760 **100**
Poole Park 11, 50, 51, 52, 53, 54, **55**, **56**, **57**, **58**, **59**, 91, **95**, **98**, 137, **140**, **141**
Poole Pottery 61, **63**, **102**
Poole Rowing Club 130
Poole Rural District Council 165, 166
Poole Waterworks Company 11, 119, 124
Poplar House 30
Portsmouth Hoy 89
Pottery Junction 149
Pound Street
  (see Baiter Street)
Powder House **122**
Precinct 16, 17, 18, **32**, **34**
Providence Street 49

Quay Railway 62, 70
Quay Street
  see Thames Street
Quays 7, 8, 17, 20, **21**, 39, 53, **60**, 61, **62**, **63**, **64**, **65**, 66, 68, 69, 70, 71, 72, 73, 75, 76, **81**, 89, 101, **106**, 131, 157

175

Index

Railway	44, 89, 117, 165	
Railway – Level Crossing	39, 48, 99	
Railway – Station	51, 52, 53, 54, 89, 93	
Railway Hotel	137	
Railway Hotel – Broadstone	165, 170, 171	
Rectory, Hamworthy	157, 160	
Red Lion Coffee House see Custom House		
Red Lion Hotel, Hamworthy	163	
Reeves, Harry	73	
Result – Schooner	79	
Ridout Family	101	
Rising Sun Inn	101, 106	
Rolles, Samuel	49	
Rose Farm, Broadstone	170	
Round House see Toll House		
Round Island	75	
Royal Bath Hotel, Bournemouth	51, 55	
Royal Mail Coach	88, 89	
Russell, Lord John	9	
Salt Water Lake	57	
Saltings	117, 125	
Salvation Army Citadel	108	
Sandbanks	76, 82, 129, 130, 131, 132, 133, 134	
Sandbanks Chain Ferry	133	
Sandbanks Ferries	132, 133	
Sandbanks Road	121	
Saunders, John	115	
Scaplen, John	23	
Scaplen's Court	17, 23	
Scutt, Benjamin	21	
Shreiber, Charles	10, 13	
Shreiber, Lady Charlotte (see also Lady Charlotte Guest)	45	
Sea View	51, 52, 90	
Seldown	137	
Seldown Lane	144	
Serpentine Road	137	
Shaftesbury, Countess of	7	
Shaftesbury, Earl of	54, 158	
Sharland, Eli, 'Granfer'	165, 167	
Shutler, A.	41, 130	
Ship Inn	19	
Shipwright's Arms	64	
Simpson's Folly	127	
Skinner Street Chapel	105	
Slade Family	24, 102, 103, 117	
Sloop Hill	53	
Smith, H. P.	23	
Snook's Post Office, Longfleet	145	
Society of Poole Men	20, 23	
South Haven Inn	78	
South Street (previously Mount Street, Great Mount Street)	39	
South Western Pottery	123	
South Western Railway Company	165	
Sprat Catch	66	
Springdale House	119	
Springdale Road	170	
Springfield Road	52	
St. Andrew's Bay	85	
St. Clement's Inn	24	
St. Clement's Lane	24	
St. James' Bell-Ringers	27	
St. James' Church	9, 13, 17, 28, 31, 45, 53	
St. James' Close	27	
Saint James' Sabbath Schools	29	
St. Joseph's Convent	141	
St. Mary's Church – Longfleet	137, 141	
St. Mary's Church, Brownsea Island	87	
St. Mary and St. Philomena Roman Catholic Church	112	
St. Michael's Church, Hamworthy	157, 160	
St. Paul's Church	45	
Stanley Green	137	
Star Hotel	41	
Station Road, Broadstone	165, 170, 171	
Steam Packet Inn	63	
Strand Street	101	
Stromboli Hill	118, 124	
Swimming Baths – Open Air	140	
Sydenham's Timber Pond	161	
Tatnam	137	
Temperance Hall	113	
Temperance Hotel	137	
Thames Street (previously Quay Street)	17, 18, 20, 24, 26, 53, 101	
Thatched Cottages	43, 146	
Thomas Kirk Wright – Lifeboat	82	
Thompson's, Peter, House	101	
Tilsed, 'Finn'	72	
Timber-Framed Houses	29	
Toll House – Longfleet	139, 142	
Topp's Corner	138	
Town Cellars (previously King's Hall and Woolhouse)	19, 20, 24, 61	
Town Gate	137, 157	
Towngate Street	39, 44, 137	
Tram Depot	90, 94-95	
Tram Terminus	99, 139	
Tramways	89, 90, 91, 92, 94, 95, 96, 97, 98, 99, 145, 152	
Turberville Family	157	
Turner, Dr. W	24	
Usher's Brewery	103	
Van Raalte, Charles	87, 131	
Van Schepdael, Edmund	50, 54	
Victoria, Queen, Jubilee	11, 51, 117, 118, 173	
Villano	85	
Wallisdown Road	149	
War Memorial – Poole Park	59	
Wareham Channel	75	
Water Gate	24	
Waterman, Mr.	165, 173	
Waterwitch – Brigantine	79	
Watkins, E.	172, 173	
Waugh, Col. and Mrs.	11, 85, 87	
Webb, Sir John	7	
Welch, Kemp, Mr.	10	
The Wellington – Mail Coach	89	
Wellington House	35	
Wessex Industries	32, 34	
Wessex Shipyard	81	
West End House	17, 101	
West Hill	126	
West Quay Road	39, 70, 111	
West Street	17, 27, 39, 53, 101, 102, 103, 104	
Weston Family	21, 24	
Weston House	45	
Weston Lane	45	
Wheeler, William	166, 168-169, 173	
White House Laundry	140	
Whitecliff	122	
'White's Place	49	
Wildfowling Punt	66, 75, 78	
Wimborne	89, 93, 165	
Wimborne, Lord see Guest, Sir Ivor Bertie		
Wimborne Road	137, 139, 146	
Wimborne Station	51	
Woolhouse see Town Cellars		
Woolworths	39, 43	
Workhouse	137	
Yacht Inn see Guildhall Tavern		
York Road	165, 172	

The drawings of the buildings in the Old Poole streets and the block plan of the Town Cellars are reproduced by permission of the Royal Commission on Historical Monuments.

ERRATUM, Page 24, line drawing; for 'King's Head' read 'King Charles'.

PLAN of the TOWN AND COUNTY OF THE TOWN OF POOLE 1841.